Really Simple PARTY CAKES

Really Simple PARTY CAKES

Evelyn Howe Fryatt

Illustrated by Teddy Cameron Long

A Sterling\Tamos Book

Sterling Publishing Co., Inc. New York

Library of Congress Cataloging-in-Publication Data

Fryatt, Evelyn Howe, 1939–
    Really simple party cakes / Evelyn H. Fryatt.
        p.   cm.
    Includes index.
    ISBN 1-895569-02-8
    1. Cake decorating. 2. Entertaining. I. Title.
    TX771.2.F78   1993
    641.8'653--dc20   92-26053
                                                         CIP

Canadian Cataloguing-in-Publication Data

Fryatt, Evelyn Howe, 1939–
    Really simple party cakes / by Evelyn H. Fryatt

    "A Sterling/Tamos book."
    Includes index.
    ISBN 1-895569-02-8
1, Cake decorating. 2. Cake. 3. Icings, Cake.
I. Title.

TX771.F792 1992   641.8/653   C92-097186-2

10   9   8   7   6   5   4   3   2

A Sterling/Tamos Book
First paperback edition published in 1994 by
Sterling Publishing Company, Inc.
387 Park Avenue South, New York, N.Y. 10016

TAMOS Books Inc.
300 Wales Avenue, Winnipeg, MB, Canada R2M 2S9

© 1993 by Evelyn H. Fryatt
Distributed in Canada by Sterling Publishing
℅ Canadian Manda Group, P.O. Box 920, Station U
Toronto, Ontario, Canada M8Z 5P9
Distributed in Great Britain and Europe by Cassell PLC
Villiers House, 41/47 Strand, London WC2N 5JE, England
Distributed in Australia by Capricorn Link (Australia) Pty Ltd.
P.O. Box 6651, Baulkham Hills, Business Centre, NSW 2153, Australia

Illustrations Teddy Cameron Long
Design A.O. Osen
Photos pp. 2 & 7 Walter Kaiser, Custom Images, Wpg
Kitchen p. 2 courtesy of The Kitchen Craft Connection, Wpg
Photography Doug Ritter Photography, Oak Bluff

Printed and bound in Hong Kong
All rights reserved

Sterling ISBN 1-895569-02-8 Trade
                1-895569-24-9 Paper

Evelyn Howe Fryatt (pictured on p2) has been decorating cakes as long as she can remember. First for family and friends and then professionally—she now teaches classes and gives demonstrations and seminars. She points out how easy it is to decorate special occasion cakes and offers decorating tips for beginners and those who are more experienced. Ms Fryatt studied cake decorating in Minneapolis, Minnesota, and in California, working with well known cake decorators Betty Newman May, Pat Simmons, Marie Sykes, and Roland A. Winbeckler.

Table of Contents

Really Simple Party Cakes

PARTY CAKES

If you would like to place a beautifully decorated party cake on your table to celebrate a special occasion, this is the book for you. Even if you are a novice cake decorator you can follow these step-by-step instructions to create your own masterpiece that will delight your family and friends. You need a minimum of equipment and most of the cakes can be baked in pans that you have in your own kitchen. A cake mix starts you off. Once the cake is cooled, follow the instructions for cutting the cake in the desired shape and then begin the icing decoration.

Basic steps guide you through preparing the cake, baking tips to keep the cake level, cooling the cake, cutting the shapes, professional icing tips, making cones to work with the icing, making professional icing, using decorating equipment, and icing and decorating special occasion cakes. Included in this book are detailed instructions for 26 different party cake ideas plus directions for making marshmallow place cards, chocolate novelties, Easter eggs, and a circus train that holds candies and nuts and makes a delightful centerpiece for your party table or sideboard.

Decorating cakes is easy to do if you follow these step-by-step instructions with diagrams. Your cakes will look professional but cost very little. You will find all the projects simple to complete. Some require no special decorating tools. Others need a few special pieces. You'll find that it is easy to color icing and make decorative stars and borders. Even icing roses are within your decorating powers. Your finished cakes will look gorgeous and no one will believe that you are a beginning decorator.

If you prefer not to use many decorating tools, you'll find decorating recipes that create stunning effects with very little effort. Other projects are slightly more detailed and some are easier to do if you use a range of metal decorating tips. These tips create very elaborate decorating effects. If you enjoy cake decorating you may wish to have some of these tips in your kitchen. It's not expensive if you buy only the sizes you will use most often.

As you become adept at handling the decorating materials you may wish to substitute your own creative cake shapes and decorating plans. There's no limit to variety and subject. Best of all it's creative and it's fun.

The various cakes in this book will require the use of some of the tools and supplies listed:

cake pans and loaf pans (cake tins)
doll pan (Dolly Varden tin)
tube pan (ring tin)
heart-shaped cake pan
baking strips
cake stand or boards covered with foil
doll picks
metal spatula and palette knife
art brush and pastry brush
No.10 & No.7 nails
paste colors or powders (food coloring)
lily nail set
wafer paper (rice paper)
foil squares
artificial stamens
sugar cherub, sugar eyes and decorations
dipping spoon and fork
plastic cake separators
candy thermometer
plastic-lined cloth bag
parchment sheets (greaseproof paper)
clear gel
meringue powder
glucose
assortment of decorator metal tips
coupler
assorted colors of chocolate wafers
uncooked spaghetti strands
graham wafers and ice-cream wafers
assorted hard candies, ball candies, and
M&M's or Smarties
licorice strings
coconut

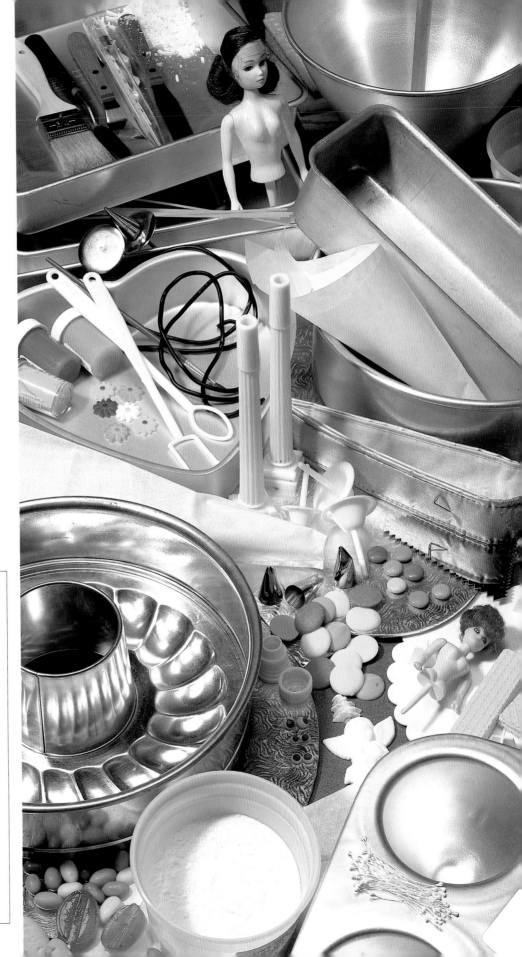

METAL TIP EQUIVALENTS

North American tip	UK/Australian tip
#13 star small	—
#16 star	#8
#17 star	#11
#18 star	#12
#22 star large	#15
#102 petal	#20 small
#103 petal	#20 medium
#104 petal	#20 large
#1 writing	#1
#2 writing	#2
#3 writing	#3
#4 writing	#4
#5 writing	—
#46 basket weave	—
#47 basket weave	#22
#48 basket weave	#23
#67 leaf	#16
#68 leaf	#17
#12 large hole	—
#349 small leaf	—
#74 leaf	—
#233 multi opening (11 holes)	—

MAKING THE CAKE

Cake mixes have been used for most of the projects in this book. They are easy to prepare and form a firm foundation for the decorating. If you prefer a homemade cake, try any of the following recipes. **Large eggs have been used for all recipes.**

Butter Cake

INGREDIENTS

½ cup	butter (at room temperature)	114g
½ tsp	vanilla flavoring	2ml
½ cup	fine white sugar	105g
2	large eggs	2
1½ cups	cake flour (sifted)	140g
1 tsp	baking powder	7g
⅓ cup	milk	75ml

Preheat oven to 325° F (160° C) electric 350° F (180° C) gas   Grease and flour pan size required for project

Using an electric mixer, beat butter and vanilla until light and creamy. Gradually add the sugar and beat until light. Add eggs, 1 at a time, beating well after each addition. Stir in half the sifted flour and baking powder and half the milk, stirring until combined. Add the remaining milk and flour and beat at medium speed until mixture is smooth. Spread into prepared baking pan and bake in preheated oven for 45 to 50 minutes or until cake tests done (p9).

Applesauce Cake

INGREDIENTS

1 cup	shortening	227g
2 cups	fine white sugar	420g
2	large eggs	2
2½ cups	flour	425g
2 tsp	cinnamon	10g
2 tsp	baking soda	7g
1 tsp	cloves	3g
½ tsp	salt	1g
1 cup	raisins	155g
1 cup	chopped walnuts or pecans	110g
2 cups	applesauce (hot)	500ml

Preheat oven to 325° F (160° C) electric 350° F (180° C) gas   Grease and flour pan size required for project

Mix together the shortening, sugar, and eggs. Sift flour, baking soda, salt, and spices together. Add to liquid mixture. Blend well. Fold in raisins and nuts. Add hot applesauce. Blend thoroughly. Pour into prepared pans and bake for 45 minutes or until cake tests done (p9).

Mother Howe's Angel Food Cake

INGREDIENTS

10	egg whites	10
1½ cups	fine white sugar	315g
1½ tsp	cream of tartar	3g
½ tsp	almond flavoring	2ml
½ tsp	vanilla flavoring	2ml
1 cup	cake flour (sifted)	95g

Preheat oven to 325° F (160° C) electric 350° F (180° C) gas   10 in tube pan (ring tin) (21cm) or doll pan (Dolly Varden tin)

Sift flour 3 times. Beat egg whites slightly, add cream of tartar, vanilla, and almond extract and beat until meringue holds soft peaks. Beat in the sugar, 2 tbs (10g) at a time, continuing to beat turning the bowl until meringue holds. Sift ¼ of flour over whites. Fold in lightly turning bowl. Fold in remaining flour by fourths. Place in ungreased tube pan (ring tin) or doll pan (Dolly Varden tin). Bake in preheated oven for 1 hour. Allow cake to hang upside down until cooled.

Marge's Never-Fail Chocolate Cake

INGREDIENTS

1 cup	butter	227g
1 cup	water	250ml
¼ cup	cocoa	20g
2 cups	all purpose (regular) flour	340g
1½ cups	fine white sugar	315g
½ tsp	salt	1g
4	large eggs	4
1 cup	commercial sour cream	250g
1 tsp	baking soda	4g

Preheat oven to 325° F (160° C) electric 350° F (180° C) gas   Grease and flour pan size required for project

Combine butter, water, and cocoa in a medium saucepan and bring to a boil. Simmer for 2 minutes. Add flour, sugar, and salt and stir well. Remove from heat and add the eggs which have been mixed with the sour cream and baking soda and beat until smooth. Pour batter into prepared baking pan and bake in preheated oven 45 to 50 minutes or until cake tests done (p9).

Plan to make the cake the day before the party. Day-old cakes are easier to cut, ice, and decorate because they don't crumb so easily. If you prefer, cakes can be made up to a month in advance and stored in the freezer in air-tight bags. Allow frozen cake to thaw in the refrigerator for 12 hours before you plan to ice it.

A 2-layer cake mix yields
    4 to 6 cups (1 to 1.5L) of batter

This will produce
    2–8-in (20.3-cm)-round layer cakes,
    1–10-in (25.4-cm)-round cake, or
    1–9 in x 13 in x 2 in
        (48cm x 33cm x 5cm) cake

Preparing Pans

Grease pans lightly with pastry brush and melted lard or shortening and flour lightly. Tap excess flour from pan.

Pans should never be filled more than 2/3 full to prevent overflow or a heavy-textured cake. Preheat oven and bake according to the instructions on the packaged mix.

Baking Pans

Select the size and shape of baking pans according to the project you are doing. You may use round or square cake pans or loaf pans. Pyrex (glass) baking dishes may also be used, but they usually require longer baking time and are difficult to time exactly. For unusual shapes you can use doll baking pans which can be purchased or rented at any cake decorating supply store. Pans in the shape of animals or cartoon characters are also available.

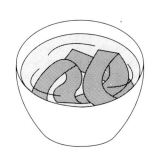
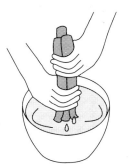
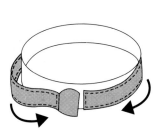
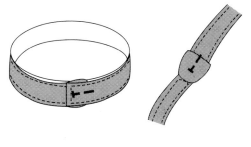

Using Baking Strips

To prevent raised centers, cracked tops, and crusty edges on the cake, use purchased reusable baking strips made of aluminized fabric. To use, soak the strips in cold water, squeeze out excess moisture, and wrap strips (aluminized side out) around the outside of the pan. Overlap the tab on strip and pin firmly in place. You may overlap and pin strips together if longer strips are needed for a larger pan. Place wrapped pans in oven and bake as directed. *Note If you use baking strips add 5 to 10 minutes to the baking time.* See done test below.

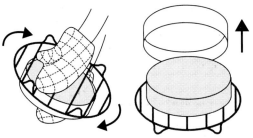

After removing the pans from the oven, remove the strips and set the pans on a cake rack. Allow the cake to cool 7 to 10 minutes. To remove the cake from the pan, place the cake rack over the cake and turn both the rack and the pan over. Carefully remove the cake.

Done Test

Cake is done when the sides begin to pull away from the pan or when a metal skewer, inserted in the center of the cake, comes out clean.

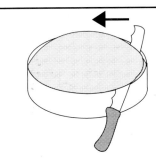

If you did not wrap the pans and your baked cake has a raised center, cut off the raise while the cake is still in the pan. Wait until the cake is slightly cool and use a serrated knife for this procedure.

To show off your finished cake and make it easier to handle or transport, place the cake on a breadboard or a specially cut piece of wood or cardboard that has been covered with foil or decorated paper. Choose a paper that has a greaseproof surface (such as foil) in a color that will suit your project.

If you don't want to cover your board, prepared boards in all sizes can be purchased at any cake decorating supply store. Smaller cakes can be placed on a cake plate, cake stand, or a suitable tray.

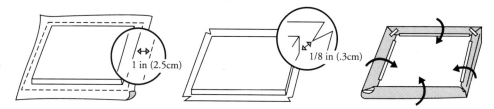

To cover the board, place the paper, pattern side down, on a flat surface and place board on top. Mark around the board with a pencil. Remove the board and allow 1 in (2.5cm) all around the marked line. Cut out. With scissors cut out a piece from each corner, as shown, 1/8 in (.3cm) from corner of board. Place board in position, fold over edges of paper, and secure with tape.

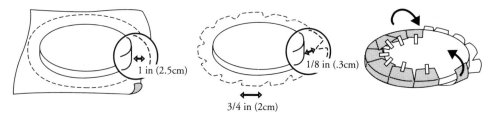

If covering a round board, repeat the procedure but make diagonal cuts with scissors ¾ in (2cm) apart all around the border to within ⅛ in (.3cm) of marked circle. Fold over border, 1 piece at a time, and secure with tape.

ASSEMBLING A 2-LAYER CAKE

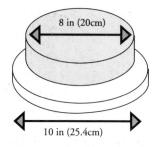

To assemble a 2-layer cake for decorating, remove 1 layer from cake rack and place it, top side up, on a cake stand or covered cake board that is 1½ in to 2 in (3.8cm to 5cm) larger than the cake.

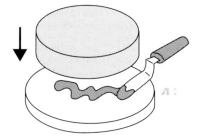

To prevent the cake from shifting, apply dab of icing to cake stand or cake board before placing the bottom cake layer. Add a ring of thick icing at this time in order to prevent the filling from seeping

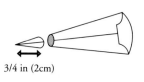

through to the icing. Make ring by half filling a large parchment (greaseproof paper) cone (p14) with Buttercream Icing (p12) and cut ¾ in (2cm) off the end of the cone.

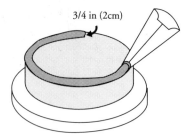

Squeeze out icing ¾ in (2cm) high around the inside edge of the cake layer.

Allow to dry. Spread filling inside ring.

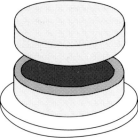

Position the top layer of the cake, bottom side up, over the filling. The cake is now ready to ice.

1. It is important to use the icing recommended for each cake design. Proper consistency plays a large part in producing professional looking cake decorations.

2. Thinned icing is used for writing, leaves, vines, outlining, and smoothing of cakes.

3. Regular icing is used for borders, flat petaled flowers, drop flowers, and figure piping.

4. Stiffened icing is used to create roses.

5. It takes 3½ cups (875 ml) icing to ice and fill an 8 in (20cm) 2-layer cake.

Choosing a Suitable Icing

Buttercream Icing

This is a good tasting creamy icing that can be made to any consistency. It is ideal for most decorating projects. It dries with a crust surface, making it good for tracing patterns. It will color well into deep shades. This icing can be stored 3 to 4 weeks in the refrigerator. It can also be frozen. Buttercream Icing can be thinned by adding corn syrup or water; however, add carefully because too much liquid will cause this icing to separate.

Decorator Icing

Buttercream Icing with the addition of meringue powder (dried egg whites) is the basic Decorator Icing. This icing allows good detail work and is ideal for decorating wedding cakes. It is excellent used over almond icing on fruit cakes. Decorator Icing can be stored in the refrigerator 2 to 3 weeks. It also makes excellent flowers and will not dry as hard as the Royal Icing. Dark colors can be obtained.

Cooked Whipped Icing

Cooked Whipped Icing is excellent for tortes, angel food cake, and sponge cake. It has the consistency of whipped cream, tastes like vanilla ice cream, is easy to spread, and can be swirled for a soft look. The frosting can be tinted if desired. Pastel shades are very pretty (it will not tint into dark colors). This icing is good for writing on cakes and making borders, but is too soft for making flowers or doing detailed decorating. However, if you use the icing, decorative touches can be added with prepared flowers, fresh flowers, or streamers. Iced cakes should be stored in the refrigerator.

Royal Icing

This icing is ideal for decorating, but not so good for eating. It is easy to work with for decorating details and dries rock hard. It is used for making icing flowers, decorating styrofoam wedding-cakes, and gluing gingerbread houses and cookies together. It can be stored in an air-tight container at room temperature for 2 weeks, but has to be beaten again before using. Deep colors can be obtained but they fade easily when exposed to bright lights.

GENERAL HINTS FOR PREPARING ICINGS

1. Beat all icings at a low to medium speed to prevent beating excessive air into the icing, making it difficult to work with.

2. Use solid white shortening and clear vanilla to ensure a snow-white icing.

3. Do not substitute butter or margarine in the Buttercream Icing recipe. The white shortening has a higher melting point, thus the warmth of your hand will not break it down as quickly, making it too soft to handle.

4. Milk can be substituted for the water but it should be scalded and cooled before using. (Icing using milk cannot be stored for any length of time.)

5. Icing made with water can be stored in the refrigerator up to 6 weeks or in a freezer for 3 to 6 months.

6. Icing sugar should be sifted for best results. Icing is better if you make it on the day the cake is to be served.

7. Be sure to apply icing so that it covers the sides of the cake around the base near the board to cover the join.

Basic Buttercream Icing

Yield: 6 cups (1.5L)

INGREDIENTS		
7½–8 cups	icing sugar	1012–1080g
½ cup	water	125ml
2 cups	solid white shortening	454g
1 tsp	clear vanilla	5ml

Using an electric mixer, mix 2 cups (270g) icing sugar, ¼ of shortening, water, and vanilla until smooth (about 5 minutes) on low speed. Add remaining shortening and icing sugar alternately and mix for 5 minutes. Scrape down sides of bowl and mix for a final 3 to 5 minutes at medium speed.

Make half the recipe for a smaller quantity.

For Chocolate Icing

Make basic Buttercream Icing recipe and add 2 tbs (7g) sifted cocoa to the icing sugar.

Poured Fondant Icing

Yield: 6 cups (1.5L)

INGREDIENTS		
½ cup (5 oz)	white wafers	126g
7 cups	icing sugar	945g
½ cup	corn syrup	125ml
½ cup	water	125ml
1 tsp	clear vanilla	5ml

Melt the white wafers using the double boiler method (p22). Using a hand-mixer at low speed blend the icing sugar, vanilla, corn syrup, water, and paste color (if you want a colored icing) together. Add this mixture to the melted wafers in the double boiler, mixing until blended.

This icing must be kept at 100°F (37.8°C) for easy pouring. Use a candy thermometer to test the temperature before pouring fondant on the cake.

This recipe will cover the 2-tier wedding cake shown on p89.

Cooked Whipped Icing

Yield: 4 cups (1L)

INGREDIENTS		
1 cup	milk	250ml
3 tbs	cornstarch (corn flour)	20g
½ cup	white margarine	114g
¾ cup	shortening	170g
1 cup	fine white sugar	210g
2 tsp	clear vanilla	5ml

Combine cornstarch (corn flour) and milk in a sauce pan. Cook over medium heat until thick, stirring slowly. Stir until cool. Combine margarine, shortening, and sugar and beat with electric mixer until creamy. This takes about 7 to 10 minutes. Add to cooled milk mixture, add vanilla, and beat until icing resembles whipped cream. This is not a sweet icing. If lumps appear in cooked cornstarch (corn flour) put mixture through blender or sieve.

Royal Icing

Yield: 3 cups (750ml)

INGREDIENTS		
4 cups	icing sugar	540g
3 tbs	meringue powder	20g
⅓ cup	water	75ml

Combine all ingredients and beat with electric mixer for 6 to 8 minutes on low speed, then 4 minutes on medium speed or until icing stands up in peaks and stiffens. This icing dries very quickly so be sure to cover the bowl with a damp cloth while you are using the icing. Utensils must be grease free. The icing breaks down with grease. If the icing becomes too thick, add a few drops of water. If it is too thin, beat in extra icing sugar. The icing may be stored in air-tight container for 2 weeks at room temperature. Beat again before using.

For smaller quantities, make half the recipe.

Decorator Icing

Yield: 2½ cups (625ml)

	INGREDIENTS	
¼ cup	white shortening	57g
1 tbs	meringue powder	7g
3 cups	icing sugar	400g
¼ cup	water	50ml
½ tsp	clear vanilla	2ml

Using an electric mixer at low speed, cream the shortening. Mix meringue powder and icing sugar together and add alternately with water to the shortening, mixing between additions. Add vanilla. Beat 5 to 7 minutes at medium speed. If the icing is too stiff, add more water; if it is too soft, add icing sugar.

No-Cook Marshmallow Frosting

Yield: 6 cups (1.5L)

	INGREDIENTS	
2	egg whites	2
¼ tsp	salt	1ml
¼ cup	fine white sugar	50g
¾ cup	light corn syrup	175ml
1¼ tsp	clear vanilla	6ml

Using electric mixer, beat egg whites and salt until soft peaks form. Add sugar gradually, beating constantly, and beat until smooth and glossy. Add vanilla. Continue beating and add corn syrup a little at a time, beating after each addition, until the frosting peaks. The finished icing has the texture and appearance of marshmallow cream.

Basic Buttercream Icing – cake shown (p36).

Poured Fondant – cake shown (p89).

Cooked Whipped Icing – cake shown (p28).

Royal Icing – lilies for cake shown (p76).

Decorator Icing – cake shown (p26).

No-Cook Marsh-mallow Frosting – cake shown (p74).

HOW TO COLOR ICING

Begin with a basic white icing recipe and add paste colors (food coloring) a little at a time using toothpicks to add the color. **Colors added to Buttercream Icing and Decorator Icing deepen in 1 to 2 hours after mixing.**

To make royal blue or red colored icings you will need larger amounts of paste color. Add the color gradually using a small metal spatula to add the color. Use extra flavoring in this icing to cover the taste of the coloring.

Be sure to mix enough icing of any one color to complete the project.

It is difficult to duplicate the exact shade of the icing color if you have not made enough the first time. **Royal Icing requires more paste color than Buttercream Icing does to achieve the same intensity.**

Paste colors may be used to color piping gel, coconut, cookie dough, marzipan, cream cheese, and cake batters. Powder colors are also available.

Always use a clean toothpick or spatula when dipping into paste colors so that the paste colors do not become contaminated with cake crumbs or icing particles.

Paste colors and powder colors are preferred to liquid colors because they can produce pastel or intense colors, as required. Liquid colors can produce only pastels. Trying to make a deeper color only adds more liquid and thins the icing making it unusable.

If paste colors become dried out, add a few drops of glycerine and stir until the color becomes smooth.

Parchment Cones

Parchment (greaseproof paper) cones make excellent decorating tools. Parchment is grease resistant, stronger than wax paper, and more pliable than freezer wrap. Parchment can be purchased at any cake decorating supply store. The sheets are 12 in x 16 in (30.5cm x 40.6cm). One sheet will make 2 large cones 12 in x 8 in (30.5cm x 20cm), 4 medium cones 6 in x 8 in (15.2cm x 20cm), or 8 small cones 6 in x 4 in (15.2cm x 10.2cm).

You may purchase parchment triangles (100 per package). Form into cone and staple edges. Clear plastic disposable ready-made cones are also available. These can be washed and used 2 or 3 times and then discarded.

Cones by themselves can be used to make decorative writing, leaves, and vines without using metal decorating tips. Refer to the diagram below for actual hole sizes for decorating cones. Holes are cut at the end of cones using sharp scissors.

Hole Sizes for Decorating Cones

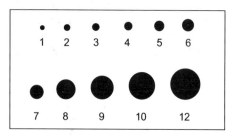

 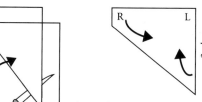

To make cones fold rectangle as illustrated and slit along fold with knife to make 2 triangles. Each will make 1 cone. Hold

 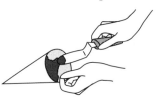

Hold the 2 points together with your right hand. Grasp the left point with your left hand and wrap the paper around cone so the point meets the

the right point of the triangle in your left hand with the point towards you. In your right hand grasp the right-hand point and curl it over until this point touches the apex point.

other 2 points. The 3 points should touch leaving no hole at the tip. Secure the edges of the cone inside and out with tape.

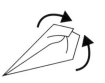 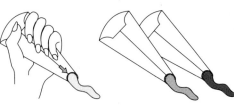

Half fill the cone with Decorator Icing (p13). Using a small metal spatula, push the icing down into the cone. (Pull the spatula out against the sides

of cone to remove icing from spatula.) Fold over ends of cone into a triangle to close. Then fold again to make a tight pouch of icing.

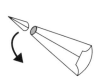 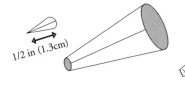 

Cut end off cone and gently squeeze cone/bag so icing moves towards the end of cone. Vary the cut at the end of the cone to make different outlines.

Cones can be refilled with icing. Use a different cone for each different color of icing.

METAL TIPS

If you plan to make fancy borders on your cake you will need metal decorating tips. You can buy the individual sizes you will use the most or a packaged set of several popular sizes and a coupler.

1/2 in (1.3cm)

To use the metal tips, cut ½ in (1.3cm) off the end of the parchment cone (wax paper will tear) and drop the tip into the cone so that half of the tip is exposed.

Half fill the cone with icing, fold over edges, and squeeze the cone bag as before.

COUPLER

A plastic coupler consisting of a ring and base, enables the decorator to change the metal decorating tips for different decorating effects while using the same color of icing in the same parchment cone.

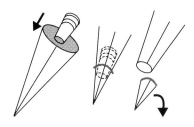

The coupler is easy to use. Simply unscrew the ring from the base and drop the base inside the parchment cone. Mark the cone where the coupler appears. Remove the coupler and cut the cone with scissors to the mark (about 1 in or 2.5cm).

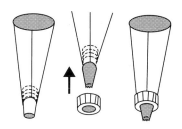

Drop the coupler back into the cone, pushing it to the end. Position the decorating tip over the coupler and screw the ring in place. To change tips, unscrew the ring and replace the tip and ring. Half fill cone with icing, fold over edges, and squeeze the cone bag.

HOW TO ICE THE CAKE

Buttercream Icing is very popular because it provides a good smooth base on which to make the decorations. To make the icing spread more easily, thin the icing with water or corn syrup until it is the consistency of whipped cream.

A very thin coat of icing will set the cake crumbs. Allow the icing to dry for 15 to 20 minutes (until dry to the touch) before proceeding with the second coat of icing. The first coat of icing will lift off the cake when you begin to apply the second coat if the first coat is not sufficiently dry. Apply second coat of icing in the same way as first coat. The second coat of icing should go on evenly, giving a smooth surface. Allow the second coat to dry 15 to 20 minutes.

Using a small metal spatula, mound the icing in the center of the cake. Spread and smooth with one way movements of the spatula, as shown.

To smooth the spatula marks, cut a circle or square of parchment the size of the top of the cake and place it on top of the cake. Run the palm of your hand back and forth over the parchment until all the lines are smoothed out.

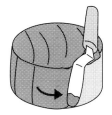

Spread icing on sides of cake and smooth around the cake with a spatula, as shown

Cut a piece of parchment as high as the cake and long enough to go around the sides of the cake. Place parchment around cake and carefully smooth with your fingers.

Do not use the above smoothing procedure on softer icing such as whipped or marshmallow, as the parchment will stick to the icing.

To smooth softer icings, use a decorating comb.

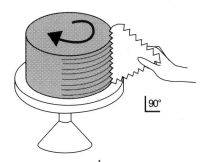

Place the iced cake on a revolving cake stand or turntable. Dip the metal comb in hot water and hold it at a 90° angle to the cake.

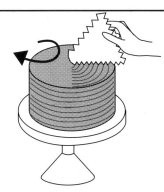

Use the same method for the top of the cake, this time holding the comb straight up from the surface of the cake as the cake revolves.

15

DECORATING TECHNIQUES

SHELLS

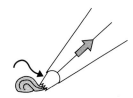

To complete shells, hold half-filled icing cone at a 45° angle to the cake, with the tip slightly above cake and end of cone pointing to the right.

Squeeze with heavy pressure and lift the tip as the icing fans out into a full shell. Ease off on the pressure as you pull the cone down towards you to make the tail of the shell. Stop the pressure and pull

the tip away. Always work towards yourself when you make shells. Start each new shell slightly behind the tail of the previous shell. Use star tip #16, #17, #18, or #22 for shells.

ZIGZAGS

To complete the zigzag, hold the half filled icing cone at a 45° angle to the cake. Touch the side of the cake slightly with the tip as you squeeze the cone in a tight up and down motion.

To finish, stop the pressure and pull the tip away. Use star tip #16, #17, #18, or #22 for zigzags.

ROPE BORDERS

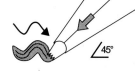
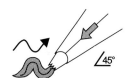

To make the border, hold the half filled icing cone at a 45° angle to the cake. The tip will touch the cake.

Move tip down and up and around to the right to form an "S" on its side. Stop the pressure on the cone and pull tip away.

Put the tip under the bottom arch of the first "S" and repeat the procedure to form a rope. Use star tip #16, #17, #18, or #22 for ropes.

RUFFLES

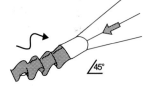
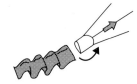
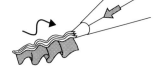

Ruffles can be completed with rose tips #104, #103, or #102. Tips #86, #87, or #88 can also be used.

If using tips #104, #103, or #102, hold the half filled icing cone at a 45° angle with the wide end of tip at the top.

If you use tip #86, #87, or #88, the star cut end of the tip will be at top of ruffle. Use an up and down motion to complete the ruffle. End by stopping the pressure and pulling hand away.

CORNELLI LACE

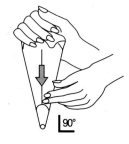

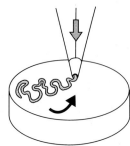

Hold the tip (use #1, #2, or #3 writing tips) slightly above the cake at a 90° angle. Use thinned icing.

Begin to squeeze the half-filled icing cone around the outside of the cake and work towards the center. Icing strings should not cross or touch.

FILL-IN STARS

Hold the half filled icing cone at a 90° angle with the tip (use star tip #16, #17, #18, or #22) slightly above the cake. Squeeze the cone. The icing that comes out will be in the form of a star. Increasing or decreasing the pressure on the cone will determine the size of star.

 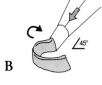 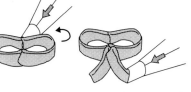

Entire cakes can be covered using this technique. The stars should be piped

very close together so that the cake is not visible between the stars.

BOWS

 A 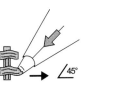 **B**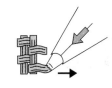

Pipe a figure "8" with writing tip #2, #3, #4, or #5. Attach an inverted "V" for the ties and add a dot of icing for the knot (A).

To form a bow using tip #104, or #103

hold the icing cone at a 45° angle to the surface of the cake with the wide end of the tip pointing straight up. While squeezing the cone move the tip up and around 1/2 of the figure "8" (B).

Repeat around the second loop on the left. Holding the cone in the same position, squeeze and return the tip to the center on both sides and then squeeze out the bow ends.

BASKET WEAVE

Use tip #46, #47, #48 or writing tip #4, #5, or #6. Hold the half-filled icing cone at a 90° angle to the cake with the serrated side of tip #46 (or other tips) facing up.

Touch the tip to the surface of the cake and squeeze out a long vertical line of icing

Hold the cone at a 45° angle to the cake and cover the vertical line with horizontal short lines each about a tip size apart.

Squeeze out another long vertical line to the right of the first line, overlapping the ends of the horizontal lines..

Again, cover the vertical line with horizontal lines, placing them into the spaces of the first row.

Repeat this entire procedure, alternating vertical lines and horizontal lines, until the area desired is covered in the basket weave pattern.

EASY POP-UP FLOWERS

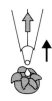

These attractive and simple-to-make flowers can be made right on the cake. Cut ½ in (1.3cm) off the end of a parchment cone and drop in tip #16.

Half fill cone with Buttercream Icing. Hold the cone and tip at a 90° angle vertical to the cake.

With the tip touching the cake, apply *very firm* pressure on the cone and allow the icing to build up at the opening of the tip onto the cake. Then pull away leaving the small mound of icing on the cake. This is a flower.

Cut ½ in (1.3cm) off the end of another parchment cone and drop in tip #13 and fill with a small quantity of yellow icing.

Squeeze a dot of icing at the center of the flower.

ICING ROSES

Most people find the making of icing roses rather intimidating, but if you follow the step-by-step directions and practice a few times it's really not so difficult. Once you've developed confidence you'll take pride in making lovely icing roses to decorate your cake. Of course it does take time. If you'd rather not undertake this task you can always buy the decorations.

Roses can be piped in several ways. You may use the No. 7 or No. 10 nails or a wooden skewer. Nails may be purchased at any cake decorating supply store.

1-1/2 in (3.8cm)

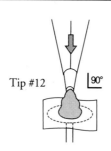

Tip #12 90°

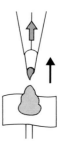

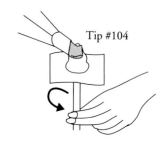

Tip #104

ROSES ON NO. 7 NAIL

Use stiffened Buttercream Icing or Decorator Icing (pp12,13) and coupler (p15) and tips #12 and #104. Attach a 1½ in (3.8cm) wax-paper square to a No. 7 nail with a dab of icing.

To make the rose mound, hold the icing cone containing tip #12 at a 90° angle to the nail and slightly above the center of the nail.

Apply heavy pressure to the cone, keeping the icing coming down the cone until you have produced a round dome-shaped mound.

Ease off the pressure as you raise the tip to form a peaked top. It is important to make a good firm dome-shaped base to support the rose petals.

Change to tip #104 to produce the petals. Hold the icing cone at a 45° angle to the nail with the narrow end of the tip slightly above the top of the mound.

It is necessary to squeeze the icing cone and turn the nail counterclockwise at the same time in order to complete a tightly wrapped ribbon of icing around the top of the peaked mound. That makes the rose bud.

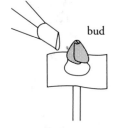

bud

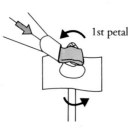

1st petal

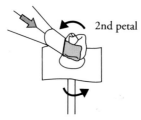

2nd petal

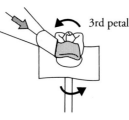

3rd petal

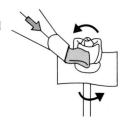

The first row of the icing rose consists of 3 petals. Hold the icing cone at a 45° angle with the wide end of tip #104 touching the base just under the ribbon of icing or bud, about midpoint of the icing mound.

To complete the first petal, turn the nail counterclockwise and move the tip up and back down to the midpoint of the bud mound.

To make the second petal, place tip #104 slightly behind the end of the first petal and pipe out the second petal in the same way as the first.

To make the third petal, place tip #104 slightly behind the end of the second petal and pipe the third petal, which will overlap the starting point of the first petal.

The second row of the icing rose con-

sists of 5 petals. The wide end of tip #104 should touch slightly below the center of a petal in the first row. Squeeze and turn the nail counterclockwise, moving the tip up and down to form the first petal in the second row.

Place tip #104 slightly behind this petal and make a second petal. Repeat the procedure until you have completed 5 petals. The last petal overlaps the first petal's starting point.

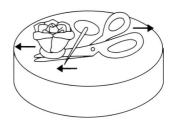

Use a small metal spatula to remove the wax paper and the rose from nail No.7.

When dry, remove rose from wax paper and place on cake. If you want to place the icing rose directly onto the cake,

use scissors instead of a metal spatula. Slide the opened scissors under the base or mound of the rose and carefully lift the rose off the wax paper square and the nail.

Set the rose on the cake by slowly closing the scissors and pushing the base of the rose with the stem end of No.7 flower nail.

ROSES ON NO.10 NAIL

You may use either stiffened Royal Icing or Buttercream Icing and flower tip #104 or #103, depending on the desired size of the finished rose. Most decorators prefer the No.10 nail because it uses less icing, is faster, and the roses are more uniform.

The No.10 nail is shaped with a peaked dome and resembles a witch hat.

Wrap a small piece of foil around the dome portion of the nail, tucking the end piece of foil under the base of the flat section of the nail to hold the foil in place and to prevent the foil from turning when you turn the nail.

Follow the instructions for roses on No.7 nail but do not make the icing mound. Instead, use tip #104 or #103 and make the icing bud with 1 swirl of icing. Carefully remove the foil and rose from the nail and let dry overnight before removing rose from foil.

ROYAL ICING ROSES ON A SKEWER

1-1/2 in (3.8cm)

1/2 in (1.3cm)

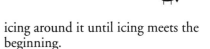

Cut ½ in (1.3cm) off the end of a parchment cone, drop in tip #104 and half fill cone with Royal Icing.

Push a 1½ in (3.8cm) wax paper square over the pointed end of a wooden skewer and slide it halfway down the skewer.

Use tip #104 and place the narrow side of tip down ½ in (1.3cm) from the top of the wooden skewer. Hold the tip parallel to the skewer, pointed directly at and a little away from the skewer. Apply pressure and twist or turn the skewer while wrapping the

icing around it until icing meets the beginning.

Move up half the width of the first icing wrap and pipe second wrap. Pipe a third wrap high enough to cover the top of the skewer. Place tip on bottom of third icing wrap and proceed to

pipe a tightly wrapped ribbon of icing around top of skewer to form the rosebud. Turn skewer and complete petals (see rose instructions p18).

When the rose on the skewer is completed, push the wax paper square under the icing rose, and carefully slide

the wax paper and the rose up and off the skewer. Royal Icing roses take at least 24 hours to dry.

19

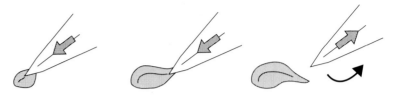

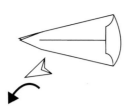

LEAVES

If you use Buttercream Icing, add water to thin the icing. The recipe for Cooked Whipped Icing (p12) is just the right consistency for making leaves.

Use a medium-size parchment cone and cut the tip to an elongated "V" or use the cone, cut off ½ in (1.3cm) from the end, and drop in tip #67, #68, #349, or #352 to make the icing leaves.

Hold the icing cone at a 45° angle to the cake surface. Squeeze the cone and

hold the tip in place in order for the icing to build up and form a base.

Then stop the pressure as you pull the tip towards you to complete the point of the leaf.

To make stand-up leaves use the same method but hold tip at a 90° angle.

LILIES

The lily nail set consists of 4 different sizes of plastic nails 2½ in (6.4cm), 1 ⅝ in (4.1cm), 1¼ in (3.2cm), and ¼ in (.6cm) in diameter. I wanted larger flowers on the Cross cake (p76) so I used the 2 larger nails. The cupped shape of the nail allows you to make natural looking flowers with turned-up petals. Royal Icing is used to form the lilies. The softer Buttercream Icing will not hold the shape.

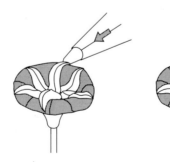

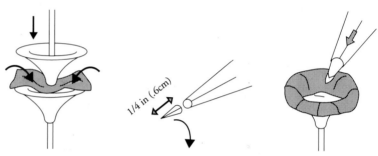

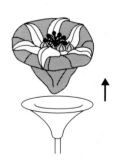

Use a 2-in (5-cm)-square piece of foil to line the bottom half of the medium-sized lily nail.

Press the top portion of the nail into the bottom half to form a foil cup.

Remove the top half.

Cut ½ in (1.3cm) off the end of a large parchment cone and insert tip #74.

Half fill cone with white Royal Icing.

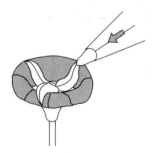

Pipe 3 evenly-spaced petals from the center of the nail. Be sure the flat side of the tip is upright. To complete each petal the pressure should be decreased as you reach the edge of the nail.

Pull the tip away to form points on the ends of the petals.

Pipe 3 additional petals between the first 3 petals, as shown.

Cut ½ in (1.3cm) off the end of a small parchment cone and insert tip #16.

Half fill cone with yellow Royal Icing and pipe stars at the center of the flower. Insert cut artificial stamens.

Gently lift the foil from the nail and allow to dry 24 hours or longer before peeling the lily off the foil and placing it on your cake.

DROP FLOWERS

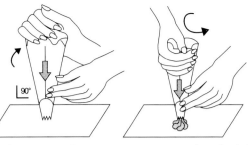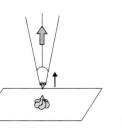

Cut ½ in (1.3cm) off the end of a large parchment cone and drop in tip #224.

Half fill cone with icing. Hold the parchment cone at a 90° angle with the tip touching the surface of the wax paper sheet.

Curve your wrist around to the left and as you squeeze out the icing return the hand to the right.

Stop squeezing and pull the tip away.

Cut ½ in (1.3cm) off the end of a medium parchment cone and drop in tip #2. Half fill cone with yellow icing.

Dot a center in flowers. Allow flowers to dry.

CAKE WRITING TIPS

1. Keep the spacing uniform between letters and words.
2. Flow letters and do not double back over lines.
3. Try to maintain good pressure control so width of squeezed line is even.
4. Be sure icing is soft but not runny.
5. Use tip #2 or #4 or cut cone to hole size 2 or 4 (p14) for most writing.
6. Practice until you are satisfied with your slant and spacing.
7. Prefer to write tall and small.
8. Be sure the spelling is accurate.
9. Hold the cone approximately 1 in (2.5cm) above cake.
   DO NOT DRAG the tip on the cake.
10. Colored piping gel works well for writing on cakes because it is just the right consistency and is easily colored with paste colors.

AaBbCcDdEeFfGgHh
IiJjKkLlMmNnOoPpQq
RrSsTtUuVvWwXxYyZz
1 2 3 4 5 6 7 8 9 0

SPAGHETTI WHISKERS

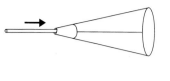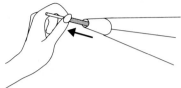

Cut off ½ in (1.3cm) from parchment cone end and insert tip #4 or #5, or cut the end off a parchment cone to size 4 or 5 hole (p14).

Half fill the cone with Royal or Buttercream Icing in the color of your choice.

Push a 5 in (12.7cm) piece of spaghetti into the open end of tip #4 or #5, or into the cut-off cone end.

Pull the spaghetti out slowly as you

squeeze the cone. Allow to dry.

The spaghetti will be evenly coated with icing and ready to use on your project.

WAFER PAPER

Wafer paper is made from potato flour, ground rice, and water and is completely edible.

Wafer paper is rough on one side. This is the DOWN side that will go next to the cake. DO NOT paint on this side. The other side is smooth. This is the UP side. Paint on this side.

Wafer paper will dissolve if it gets wet.

If you drip water or any liquid onto the paper, that spot will disintegrate.

Do not store wafer paper in a damp place. Store it in a cardboard box in a dry cupboard.

Use nontoxic felt-tipped pens or markers to trace patterns onto wafer paper. *Apply piping gel to pattern before painting.*

SUGAR DECORATIONS

Sugar flowers and other shapes can be purchased in a variety of colors and sizes ready to put on the cake. They make decorating easy.

HOW TO COLOR COCONUT

Stir a toothpick dipped in the paste color in a large spoon of milk. Place coconut in plastic bag and add colored milk to coconut. Twist bag to close and knead until coconut is evenly tinted.

Or you may use a few drops of liquid

coloring using the previous method to tint the coconut.

Or you may choose to add ¼ teaspoon (1ml) of powder coloring to a plastic bag or container with a lid. Add coconut and shake until evenly coated.

HOW TO MELT WAFERS

Wafers are round flat discs of confectionery coating. They are available in light and dark chocolate and vanilla flavors in white and seasonal colors (red, green, and yellow for Christmas, and violet and pink for spring or Easter). These wafers can be melted and used to produce molded holiday novelties and bite-size candies, chocolate-covered cookies, and ganaches or icings.

Microwave Method

To melt a pound (.45kg) of wafers, place them in a large glass measuring

cup or glass bowl and place in microwave. Use DEFROST setting for 2 minutes. Stir thoroughly, then microwave the wafers in 30-second intervals (still at DEFROST) stirring after each interval. It takes about 4 to 5 minutes to melt a pound of wafers.

Double Boiler Method

Place hot tap water in the bottom of a double boiler. Add wafers to the top of the double boiler and place over the bottom section. Allow to sit for 5 minutes, then stir. Replace hot tap water as

required to melt the wafers. DO NOT PLACE THE POT OF WATER ON THE STOVE. Overheating will cause the wafers to thicken. *Note* Chocolate may also be melted this way.

Be sure to stir the wafers occasionally while they are melting in order to blend them and provide uniform temperature. This also prevents possible streaking in the finished product.

Do not add water, milk, or any liquid to the wafers. This will make them thicken and harden immediately.

Really Simple PARTY CAKES

The following cake decorating projects are very easy. Most use a minimum of equipment; others require a few special icing tools. For example, you can decorate some cakes without using decorator tips. Instead, you can cut the ends off parchment (greaseproof paper) cones to different hole sizes according to a chart on p14 to make icing lines, writing, or vines. Or you can cut the hole in a special way (p20) to make icing leaves. If you decide to buy only one decorating tip, you can use parchment cones and star tip #18 for such decorating effects as stars, zigzags, shells, and fill-in borders. Ruffles and more intricate decorating details require the use of a variety of decorating tips. The tips are easy to use. Just follow the step-by-step instructions for spectacular looking party cakes.

Picnic Bear

INGREDIENTS

1	2-layer cake mix or Angel Food Cake (p8)	1
	Buttercream Icing (p12)	
1½ cups	dark brown	375ml
1 cup	beige	250ml
¼ cup	black	50ml
2 tbs	white	25ml
1	flat red candy for tongue	1

EQUIPMENT

1 doll pan (Dolly Varden tin)

1– 10-in (25.4-cm)-round, glass plate or covered cake board (p10)

small strip of parchment paper

4 parchment (greaseproof paper) cones: 2 large, 2 medium

paste colors: black, brown

small metal spatula

3½ in (9cm) palette knife

toothpicks

no.3 art brush

scissors

party hat

cardboard or bristol board collar

plaid bow tie (optional)

Prepare cake mix according to the instructions on the cake-mix package or use the Angel Food Cake recipe. Prepare doll pan (p9). Pour cake mixture into doll pan. Bake at 350°F (180°C) (gas or electric) for 55 to 60 minutes until cake tests done (p9). Allow cake-mix cake to stand in pan 5 minutes, then turn onto wire rack to cool. See instructions for cooling Angel cake.

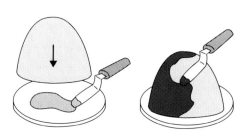

Place cooled cake on plate or covered board. Secure with a dab of Buttercream Icing. Then use a small metal spatula to apply brown icing to the entire cake. After icing dries, smooth out the spatula lines with a strip of parchment paper (p15).

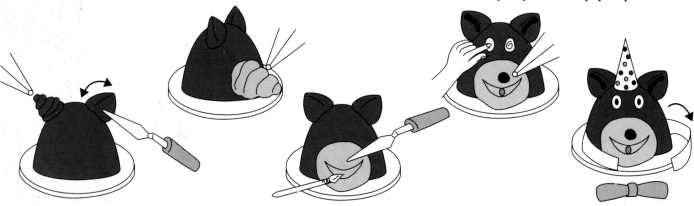

Using 1 large parchment cone, cut the end to a size 12 hole (p14), and half fill with dark brown Buttercream Icing. Pipe large mounds of icing for ears. Shape the ears with a palette knife.

Half fill another large parchment cone with beige Buttercream Icing. Cut the end to a size 12 hole (p14).

Mark the center of the face with a toothpick. This indicates the mouth area. Pipe out beige icing in large mounds 1½ in (3.8cm) from center of face. This will build up the snout. Use the palette knife to shape the snout and the front of the head. Use the art brush to shape the mouth. Add the flat red candy for the tongue.

Put white Buttercream Icing into a medium parchment cone. Cut the end to a size 4 hole (p14). Pipe 1-in (2.5-cm)-oval mounds of icing for eyes. As this dries, flatten the mounds with your finger.

Put black Buttercream Icing into the other medium parchment cone. Cut the end to a size 4 hole (p14). Draw lines on bear ears with the black icing and add black pupils to the eyes. Mound the icing into a ball shape for the nose. When the pupils and nose dry, flatten the pupils with your finger and shape the nose.

Cut out strip of thin cardboard or bristol board to fit around neck. Tape closed. Add bow tie and party hat.

Easter Bunny

INGREDIENTS		
2-layer cake mix	1	1
Buttercream Icing (p12) or Decorator Icing (p13)		
3 cups	white	750ml
¼ cup	pink	50ml
dab	cornstarch	dab
3 strands	uncooked spaghetti	3 strands
2	red Smarties or M&M's	2

EQUIPMENT

1 doll pan (Dolly Varden tin)

1– 10-in (25.4-cm)-round glass plate or
   covered cake board (p10)

pink bristol board (for ears) 5 in x 7 in
   (12.5cm x 18cm)

ear pattern (p92)

2 parchment (greaseproof paper) cones:
   1 large, 1 medium

tips #5, #18

paste color: pink

glue

*The day before the cake is to be
served—* cut out the ears from the
bristol board using ear pattern. Glue
toothpicks to the back of ears, as
shown. Allow to dry overnight.

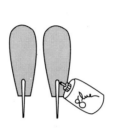  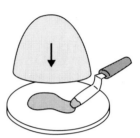 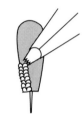

Prepare cake mix according to the
instructions on the cake-mix package.
Prepare the pan (p9) and bake at 350°F
(180°C) (gas or electric) for 45 to 60
minutes or until cake tests done (p9).
Cool cake in pan on a wire rack.

On the day of the party— spread a
dab of icing in the center of covered
cake board and invert cooled cake
onto board.

Cut ½ in (1.3cm) off the end of the
large parchment cone and drop tip
#18 (star) inside. Half fill with white
icing.

Push out long stars of icing over the
surface of the cake until the top and
sides are completely covered and look
like fur. Push out more stars to build
up icing over bunny's cheeks. Push out
2 rows of stars around the front edge
of ears, as shown.

 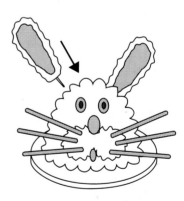

Add the pink icing to the medium
parchment cone and cut off the end of
the cone to size 5 hole (p14) or add tip
#5 to cone before adding icing.
Squeeze pink piping for eyes, nose,
and tongue.

Flatten the pink piping with your
finger dipped in cornstarch.

Add red candies for the eyes, as shown.

Make spaghetti whiskers (p22) and
position on bunny for whiskers, as
shown.

Position bunny ears with toothpicks,
as shown.

Holiday Wreath

INGREDIENTS		
1	2-layer cake mix or Applesauce Cake (p8)	1
2 cups	Cooked Whipped Icing (p12)	500ml
30	spearmint leaves	30
22	cinnamon hearts	22
15	silver dragees	15
3	red licorice strings	3

EQUIPMENT

1– 10 in (25.4cm) tube or bundt pan (ring tin)
1– 12 in (30cm) cake plate or
   covered cake board (p10)
small metal spatula
1 large parchment (greaseproof paper) cone
tip #18

Prepare the cake mix according to the instructions on the cake-mix package or use Applesauce Cake recipe. Prepare the baking pan (p9). Bake at 325°F (gas 180°C, electric 160°C) for 30 to 35 minutes or until cake tests done (p9). Allow cake to cool in pan 5 to 7 minutes, then turn onto a cake rack to cool.

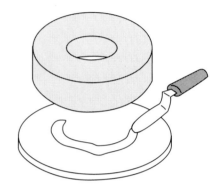

Once cake is cooled, secure it to the cake plate with dabs of Cooked Whipped Icing. Ice the entire cake with the icing using the small metal spatula. Cut ½ in (1.3cm) off end of a large parchment cone. Insert tip #18 and half fill with white icing.

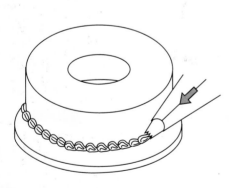

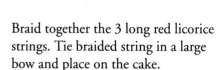

Complete a shell border (p16) around the base of the cake.

Decorate the top of the cake with spearmint leaves. Add red candies, and silver dragees (decorator's silver candy balls).

Braid together the 3 long red licorice strings. Tie braided string in a large bow and place on the cake.

Valentine Heart

INGREDIENTS		
1	2-layer yellow cake mix	1
2 cups	Cooked Whipped Icing (p12)	500ml
7	red heart-shaped gumdrops	7
14	cinnamon hearts	14
3 tsp	red sugar sprinkles	5g
3	sugar cherubs: 2 small, 1 large	3

EQUIPMENT
1– 8-in (19-cm)-square cake pan
1– 8-in (19-cm)-round cake pan
1– 14-in (35-cm)-round covered
  cake board (p10)
baking strips
serrated knife
tips #16, #86 (or only tip #18)
coupler (optional)
1 large parchment (greaseproof paper) cone
6 in (15cm) heart pattern (p92)
small metal spatula
wax paper
toothpicks

Prepare the cake mix according to the instructions on the cake-mix package. Measure 2½ cups (625ml) of batter into the round baking pan and 3 cups (750ml) of batter into the square baking pan. Wrap pans with baking strips and bake at 350°F (180°C) (gas or electric) for 25 to 30 minutes or until cake tests done (p9).

Remove baking strips and cool the cakes in the pans on a cake rack for 7 minutes. Then invert the cakes onto cake rack and allow to cool completely.

Using a serrated knife, cut the round cake in half. Position the cakes on the covered cake board to form a heart. Secure them to the board with a dab of icing.

Ice the cakes together, as shown, using metal spatula. Smooth top icing with spatula. Chill cake in refrigerator to set icing.

Trace heart pattern on wax paper. Cut out. Place this pattern on the center of the cake and trace around it with a toothpick. Remove the pattern.

Fill in the traced heart with red sugar sprinkles. Position the heart-shaped gumdrops and cinnamon hearts, as shown.

Cut 1 in (2.5cm) off the end of a large parchment cone and drop in a coupler. Attach tip #16 and half fill the cone with Cooked Whipped Icing. Zigzag icing (p16) around bottom edge of

cake (or use tip #18 without a coupler). Using the same tip (#16 or #18), make a shell border (p16) around the top edge of cake.

Using the same cone of icing, remove

tip #16 and replace it with tip #86 to make ruffles (p16) around the red heart. If you use tip #18 you will make zigzags (p16) instead of ruffles.

Place large cherub and 2 smaller cherubs on red heart, see photograph.

Baby Shower

INGREDIENTS		
2	2-layer cake mixes	2
8 cups	Cooked Whipped Icing (p12) blue *(make 2 recipes)*	2L
1 pkg	sugar decorations (for a baby)	1 pkg
1 pkg	sugar blossoms	1 pkg
1	sugar daisy	1

EQUIPMENT

1– 11 in x 15 in x 2 in
  (27.5cm x 37.5cm x 5cm) baking pan
1– 20-in (50-cm)-round covered
  cake board (p10)
baking strips
serrated knife
3-in (7.6-cm)-round biscuit cutter
toothpicks
1 large parchment (greaseproof paper) cone
tip #18
paste color: blue
2 yds (2 m) ¼-in (.6-cm)-wide white ribbon
1 pattern for baby sweater (p92)
wax paper

Prepare the cake mixes according to the instructions on the cake-mix packages. Prepare the baking pan (p9). Add cake mixture and wrap the pan with baking strips (p9). Bake at 350°F (180°C) (gas or electric) for 45 minutes or until cake tests done (p9). Remove baking strips and cool in pan on a wire rack for 7 minutes. Remove cake from pan and invert on the covered board, using a dab of icing on the board to keep the cake in

place. Cut out sweater pattern from wax paper. Place it on cake and cut around it carefully with a serrated knife. Remove the round neck portion and position it with icing on the board for the bonnet.

Cut the front of the booties from the leftover side pieces of cake using the biscuit cutter. Position these pieces with icing on the board. Use the cut-off rectangular top pieces of cake and position them behind bootie circles, as shown. Ice bootie parts together with a thin layer of icing.

Use a toothpick to mark a collar around the cut-out neck, as shown.

Make 2 shell borders 1 in (2.5cm) apart at bonnet edge. Fill in bonnet and around edges with zigzags. Make shell border around top edge of booties and toe edge. Fill in with zigzags. Zigzag side edges of bonnet and booties, as in sweater.

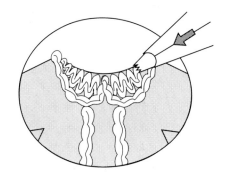

Cut ½ in (1.3cm) off the end of a large parchment cone, insert tip #18. Half fill cone with blue icing. Outline the collar and down the front with plain shells (p16). Complete the inside section of the collar with large zigzags (p16).

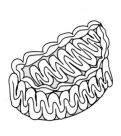

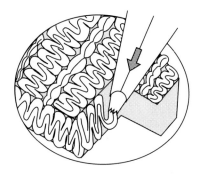

Space rows of plain shells (p16) 1 in (2.5cm) apart down the sweater, working from center front edges and down sleeve sides. Using the same tip fill in the spaces with zigzags. Using this decorating procedure, the completed outfit will appear to have a knitted finish. Also zigzag bottom, neck, and sleeve edges of the cake.

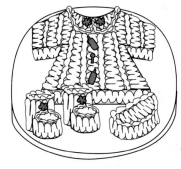

Add baby sugar decorations to the front of the sweater and sugar blossoms to the booties and around the collar and down the front.

Cut the ribbon into 2 – 12 in (31cm) lengths and make bows for the booties. Cut a 16 in (41cm) ribbon length and make a bow for neck. Cut 2 – 15 in (38cm) ribbons for bonnet tails and secure the ribbon to the bonnet with a sugar daisy, as in photograph above.

33

Easter Egg Cookies

INGREDIENTS		
1 cup	peanut butter (smooth)	260g
1 cup	margarine	227g
1 cup	brown sugar (firmly packed)	175g
2	eggs	2
2 tsp	vanilla	10ml
3 cup	all-purpose flour (regular flour)	510g
½ tsp	salt	1g
½ tsp	cinnamon	3g
1½ lb	pastel-colored chocolate wafers	.68kg
sugar novelties for flowers & leaves or use Buttercream Icing (p12) to create your own		

EQUIPMENT

1 ungreased cookie sheet
foil or parchment (greaseproof) paper sheet
dipping spoon
straw basket
cellophane grass

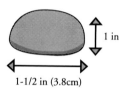
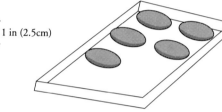

In a large mixing bowl, cream the peanut butter with the margarine. Gradually add the sugar. Beat in eggs and vanilla. Sift together the flour, salt, and cinnamon and stir into the mixture. Chill for 1 hour.

Shape the dough into 1½ in (3.8cm) long and 1 in (2.5cm) thick egg shapes.

Place on ungreased cookie sheet and bake at 375°F (180°C electric, 190°C gas) for 8 to 10 minutes. *Note Larger cookie egg shapes require longer baking time.* Allow the cookies to cool.

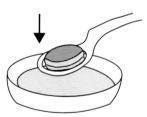

Melt the pastel-colored chocolate wafers (p22). Place the bottoms of the cookie eggs into the melted chocolate. Set them on a sheet of foil or parchment paper. They will harden and will have a bottom. When the bottom is set, place the cookie egg on a dipping spoon and

dip it into more melted wafers, coating the egg completely. As you remove the egg and spoon, tap the spoon on the side to remove excess coating from the egg. Set the egg, bottom side down, on the sheet of foil or parchment. Allow to set. Cover all the cookie eggs in this

way. Use different colored wafers to create a variety of colored eggs. Eggs may be decorated with sugar novelties or Buttercream Icing flowers and leaves (p20, 21).

Place eggs in a straw basket that has been lined with cellophane grass.

Clown

EQUIPMENT

1–10 in (25.4cm) heart cake pan, **or use**
   1– 8-in (20-cm)-round and 1– 8-in (20-cm)-
   square pan (cut round cake in half and place
   with square cake to make heart)
1– 14-in (35-cm)-round covered
   cake board (p10)
baking strips
parchment (greaseproof) paper
paste colors: yellow, green, red, orange
4 parchment(greaseproof paper) cones:
   3 large, 1 medium
3 couplers
tips #104, #18, #4, #16, #14
small metal spatula
toothpicks

Note If you have only tip #18 you may use this for all the decorating. Instead of ruffles for the collar, you will make zigzags (p16). You will need separate cones for each color of icing. Use red icing in a medium parchment cone and cut the end to a size 4 hole (p14) to outline mouth. In another cone use tip #18 to fill in the mouth with red icing. Cut end off another medium parchment cone to size 4 hole (p14) and add green icing. Outline eyes and make eyebrows. Fill in eyes with yellow icing in small parchment cone.

	INGREDIENTS	
1	2-layer cake mix	1
	Buttercream Icing (p12)	
2 cups	white	500ml
1 cup	yellow	250ml
½ cup	green	125ml
½ cup	orange	125ml
¼ cup	red	50ml
6	tiny sugar blossoms	6
2	small green candies	2
2	flat oval yellow gum-type candies	2
1	large red gum ball	1

Prepare cake mix according to the instructions on the cake-mix package. Grease the heart pan. Pour the cake mixture into the pan and wrap pan with baking strips (p9). Bake at 350°F (180°C) (gas or electric) for 35 minutes or until cake tests done (p9). Allow cake to stand in pan 5 to 7 minutes. Invert the cake onto a large cake rack and cool completely. Place a dab of icing on the covered board and invert the cooled cake onto the board.

Using a small metal spatula, ice cake with white Buttercream Icing, smoothing top and sides (p15).

Cut 1 in (2.5cm) off the end of a large parchment cone and drop in coupler. Attach tip #104 and half fill the cone

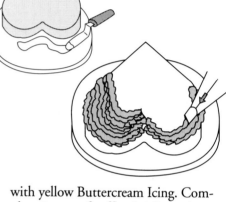

with yellow Buttercream Icing. Complete 8 rows of ruffles (p16) starting at the bottom center of the cake with the first ruffle and working up one side, then the other, as shown. Overlap each row of ruffles until collar is completed.

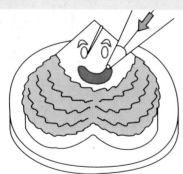

With a toothpick mark eyes, eyebrows, nose, and wide mouth. Cut 1 in (2.5cm) off the end of a medium cone and drop in a coupler. Add tip #4 and put in red Buttercream Icing. Outline the mouth and draw a center line. Change tip to #16 and fill in the mouth with fill-in stars (p17).

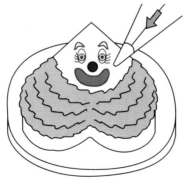

Position the yellow and green candies and red gum ball on the face with dabs of icing. Cut 1 in (2.5cm) off large cone, drop in coupler, attach tip #4 and add green Buttercream Icing to outline eyes and make inverted V-shaped eyebrows Add eyelashes with the same tip. Change to tip #14 on the

yellow icing cone and fill in eyebrows with small fill-in stars (p17).

Use a toothpick to draw a bow tie on the lower portion of the ruffled cake. Using green icing cone, change to tip #16 or #18 to fill in the bow tie with icing stars. Add small sugar blossoms to the tie.

Cut ½ in (1.3cm) off a large parchment cone and insert tip #18. Fill with orange icing. Using this tip, pull out long stars (p17) of icing for the clown's hair.

Father's Day

INGREDIENTS		
1	2-layer cake mix	1
	Buttercream Icing (p12)	
3 cups	white	750ml
½ cup	red	125ml
½ cup	blue	125ml
¼ cup	brown	50ml
dab	cornstarch	dab

EQUIPMENT

1– 9 in x 13 in (22.8cm x 33cm) cake pan

baking strips

1– 10 in x 14 in (25.4cm x 35.5cm) covered
   cake board (p10)

4 parchment (greaseproof paper) cones:
   1 small, 3 medium

tips #4, #16, #18, #5, #1, #48

4 couplers

paste colors: red, blue, brown

small metal spatula

toothpicks

ruler

collar and vest pattern (p92)

Note If you have only tip #18 you may
use this for all the decorating. You will
have to change the icing cones each time
you change the colors. Cut the end off a
small parchment cone to size 4 hole (p14)
and use brown icing to trace diamond
lines and message on tie. Trace around
collar and tie. Using different cones and
red, blue, and white icings, fill in
diamonds, as described in directions. Pipe
a mound of white icing for the buttons
and small brown dots for the button eyes.
Make shell border, as described.

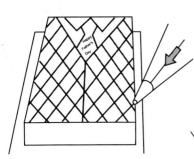

brown icing. Follow the lines of the
printed message, "Happy Father's
Day." Also pipe line around collar and
tie and the lines to make diamond
shapes on vest. Cut off 1 in (2.5cm)
from the ends of the 3 medium
parchment cones, drop a coupler into
each cone, and fill each with icing: one
red, one blue, and one white.

38

Prepare the cake mix according to the
instructions on the cake-mix package.
Prepare the baking pan (p9). Add cake
mixture and wrap the pan with baking
strips (p9). Bake at 350°F (180°C) (gas
or electric) for 35 minutes or until cake
tests done (p9). Remove baking strips.
Cool in pan on a wire rack 5 to 7 minutes. Remove cake from pan and invert
on the covered board, using a dab of
icing to hold cake in place. Ice sides
and top of cake with white icing using
a metal spatula. Smooth with

parchment. After the
icing has dried, lay the collar pattern
on top of the cake and trace around it
with a toothpick. Remove pattern.

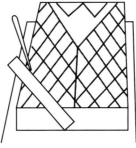

Measure 1 in (2.5cm) from each side at
the top of the cake. Lay vest pattern on
cake and trace around with toothpick.
Extend a line from the center of "V" to
the bottom of the cake for vest opening.
Use a ruler and toothpick and carefully
mark lines on the cake at 1 in (2.5cm)

intervals, as shown. This will form the
diamond pattern. Draw the tie and
center message with a toothpick.

Cut off 1 in (2.5cm) from the end of a
small parchment cone, insert coupler
and add tip #4. Half fill cone with

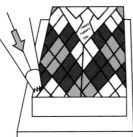

Add tip #16 to each coupler in turn,
and make fill-in stars (p17) on the cake
between brown lines to fill in diamonds.
When you are using the red icing cone

make red stripes across tie (see photograph). Change the tip on the blue
icing cone to #48 and pipe "V" section
of sweater and down front opening.

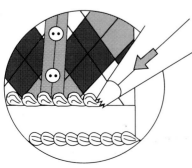

Change the white Buttercream Icing cone to tip #5 and pipe white icing balls for buttons. Allow the balls to dry and flatten them with your finger dipped in cornstarch to resemble a button. Change the tip on the cone of brown icing to #1 and draw a brown circle on the button and 2 eyes for the buttonholes. Make shell borders (p16) around top and bottom of cake using the white icing cone and tip #18.

Christmas Tree

EQUIPMENT
1– 9 in x 13 in (19cm x 29cm) cake pan
baking strips
1 oval covered cake board (p10) or
  board cut using tree pattern
2½ in (6.8cm) star cookie cutter
paste colors: green, yellow, brown
Merry Christmas decal
4 parchment (greaseproof paper) cones: 2 large,
  2 medium
tips #18, #74, #16, #17
toothpicks
1 paper doily
1 tree pattern (p93)

Note You may use a parchment cone for putting on green icing; cut the end for leaves (p20).

You may use tip #18 and separate parchment cones for icing colors, reusing tip #18 as needed.

INGREDIENTS		
1	2-layer cake mix or	1
	Never-Fail Chocolate Cake (p8)	
	Buttercream Icing (p12)	
3 cups	dark green	750ml
¼ cup	yellow	50ml
¼ cup	light brown	50ml
½ cup	white	125ml
1	candy cane sugar add-on	1
	Smarties or M&M's	
5	red	5
10	yellow	10
6	green	6

Prepare the chocolate cake mix according to the instructions on the cake-mix package or use the Never-Fail Chocolate Cake recipe. Prepare the baking pan (p9). Add cake mixture and wrap pan with baking strips (p9). Bake at 350°F (180°C) (gas or electric) for 30 to 35 minutes or until cake tests done (p9). Allow the cake to stand in pan 5 to 7 minutes, then carefully invert cake onto a cake rack to cool. Wrap and freeze cake.

Cut the frozen cake into a large tree using pattern. Cut the 2½ in (6.8cm)

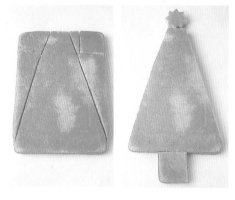

star for the top of the tree with a star cookie cutter and also cut a 2¾ in (7cm) square for the tree trunk. These are cut from the leftover side pieces of cake.

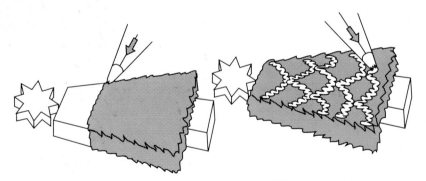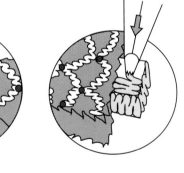

Assemble cake on white doily placed on board and adhere with a dab of icing. Ice pieces together. Cut ½ in (1.3cm) off the end of a large parchment cone, insert tip #74 (leaf), and half fill cone with green icing. Completely cover tree shape with green icing leaves. Start at the base of the tree and work upward. Allow to dry.

With a toothpick mark garlands on the iced cake. Cut ½ in (1.3cm) off a large parchment cone, insert tip #18, and half fill cone with white icing. Zigzag (p14) to complete the garlands. Add flat candies to garlands (see photo).

Cut ½ in (1.3cm) off the end of a medium parchment cone, add tip #16, and half fill cone with yellow icing.

Fill in the star. Using another medium parchment cone, cut off end, add tip #17 and fill with light brown icing. Fill in tree trunk. Pipe zigzag borders on edges of star and trunk using the same cones. Place flat candies on tree trunk and the sugar candy cane on the star. Place the Merry Christmas decal on tree.

Butterfly

INGREDIENTS		
1	2-layer cake mix or Applesauce Cake (p8)	1
2 cups	Cooked Whipped Icing (p12)	500ml
	Buttercream Icing (p12)	
1 cup	mauve or violet	250ml
1 cup	purple	250ml
	black licorice string (for antennae)	

EQUIPMENT

1– 10 in (25.4cm) bundt pan or tube pan (ring tin)
1– 14-in (35.6-cm)-round cake board or
   glass plate
metal spatula
palette knife
toothpicks
2 large parchment (greaseproof paper) cones
tip #16, #18
paste colors: mauve, purple

Note Buttercream Icing must be used for the purple icing on this cake. Dark colors cannot be obtained using the Whipped Icing.

Prepare cake mix according to the instructions on the cake-mix package or use the Applesauce Cake recipe. Prepare the baking pan (p9). Add the cake mixture and bake at 325°F (160°C electric or 180°C gas) for 30 to 35 minutes or until cake tests done (p9). Allow cake to cool in pan 5 to 7 minutes, then carefully invert onto a cake rack to cool completely.

Cut the cake in half and place halves on board, as shown. Secure to board or stand with icing. Ice cake using Cooked Whipped Icing and a metal spatula.

Cut ½ in (1.3cm) off the end of a large parchment cone and insert tip #16. Half fill the cone with purple Buttercream Icing. Using a toothpick mark a 1-in (2.5-cm) -oval shape at the center of the cake and a center line on each side of this oval, as shown. Draw 4

more oval shapes for wing centers, as shown. Outline the wing ovals and fill in the center oval with purple icing stars. Using the same tip #16 and the purple icing, complete a zigzag border (p16) around the top of the cake and down the corners and on center

horizontal line. Using the other parchment cone cut ½ in (1.3cm) off the end, insert tip #18 and fill with mauve icing. Make mauve icing zigzags around the center oval (butterfly body). Make mauve icing stars to fill

purple wing center ovals. Outline the wing center ovals with mauve using a zigzag motion and the same cone and
42

tip. Continue to make zigzag mauve lines of icing on each side of center purple lines on the butterfly cake. Add mauve zigzag icing borders at the

bottom of the cake. Cut 2 pieces of licorice about 5 in (13cm) long. Insert licorice antennae into the top of the cake. Add a purple icing star to the ends of the licorice to complete the antennae.

Baby Bib

INGREDIENTS		
1	2-layer white cake mix	1
	Buttercream Icing (p12)	
3 cups	white	750ml
2 cups	pink	500ml
¼ cup	clear gel	50ml

EQUIPMENT

1– 9 in x 13 in (22.9cm x 33cm) baking pan

1– 10 in x 14 in (25.4cm x 35.6cm)
 covered cake board (p10)

baking strips

3½-in (9-cm)-diameter wax paper circle

3 parchment (greaseproof paper) cones:
 1 small, 2 large

tips #14, #104, #18

2 couplers

paste color: pink

3 in (7.6cm) circle of wax paper

6 in (15cm) square of wax paper

bunny pattern (p92)

toothpicks

Note If you use only tip #18, the ruffle border around bib will be replaced with a zigzag border (p16).

Tape wax paper square over the bunny pattern. Color the gel with a speck of pink paste color on the end of a toothpick. Place colored gel in a small cone and cut a size 1 hole (p14) at the end of cone. Squeezing out a continuing line, quickly trace the picture on the wax paper, as shown. *Gel should not dry.* Lift the wax paper, turn over, and line it up over the top of the cake. Lower

Prepare the cake mix according to the instructions on the cake-mix package. Prepare the cake pan (p9). Pour the cake mixture into the pan and wrap pan with baking strips (p9). Bake at 350°F (180°C) (gas or electric) for 30 to 35 minutes or until cake tests done (p9). Remove baking strips and cool pan on a wire rack. Remove cake from pan, place on wire rack, and allow to cool completely. Cover top and sides with 2 cups (500ml) white icing. Smooth out (p15).

the wax paper onto the cake and lightly rub the gel lines with a toothpick. Lift the wax paper off the cake. Using the cone of pink gel, retrace the bunny outline on the cake and fill in the center of ear, nose, and eye. If necessary cut a

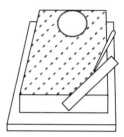

Place wax paper circle at top of cake, as shown. Trace around it with a toothpick. With a ruler and toothpick mark broken diagonal lines across the cake 1 in (2.5cm) apart, as shown.

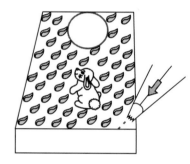

slightly larger hole, size 2 (p14), at the cone end to create smooth lines.

Cut 1 in (2.5cm) off the end of a large parchment cone. Insert the coupler and attach tip #14. Half fill the cone with pink icing. Pipe shells ½ in (1.3cm) apart to form a pattern following the diagonal trace lines.

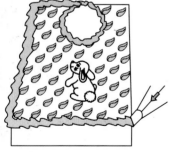

Using the same cone change to tip #104 and complete a ruffle border (p16) around the outside of the cake to form the bib.

Trace a figure 8 with toothpick on bib

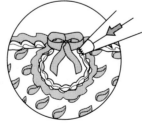

(p17) for bow. Using the same tip and pink icing cone, follow the tracing to make the bow.

Cut 1 in (2.5cm) off the end of the other large parchment cone. Insert a

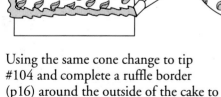

coupler and attach tip #14. Half fill the cone with white icing and pipe small shells (p16) on the inside of the pink ruffle. Change to tip #18 and make large shells around the bottom border.

Shamrock

INGREDIENTS		
1	2-layer cake mix	1
	Cooked Whipped Icing (p12)	
2 cups	pale green	500ml
	Buttercream Icing (p12)	
1 cup	dark green	250ml

EQUIPMENT

3 – 6 in (15.2 cm) heart-shaped
   baking pans or cut hearts from
   11 in x 15 in (27.9cm x 38.1cm)
   cake using heart pattern (p92)
1– 14-in (35.6-cm)-round covered
   cake board (p10)
baking strips
tips #2, #16, #18
1 coupler
paste color: green
2 large parchment (greaseproof paper) cones
3 – 8-in (20-cm)-round doilies
pencil
stem of shamrock pattern (p93)

Note If you have only tip #18 use it with
a parchment cone and dark green icing
to make shells around top borders and
for fill-in stars on stem. The lacy pattern
on the top of the cake can be made with
a cone with end cut to size 2 hole (p14).

Prepare the cake mix according to the
instructions on the cake-mix package.
Prepare the cake pans (p9). Divide cake
mixure evenly among the 3 heart pans
or use 1 oblong pan. Wrap pans with
baking strips (p9). Bake oblong pan at
350°F (180°C) (gas or electric) for 45
minutes or heart pans for 25 minutes
or until cakes test done (p9). Remove
baking strips and cool pans on a wire
rack 5 to 7 minutes. Remove from pans
and invert cakes onto a wire rack to cool
completely. Wrap and freeze oblong
cake. Use pattern to cut out hearts.

Position the 3 heart-shaped cakes on the
covered board using a dab of icing to
hold the cakes in place. Doilies should
first be adhered to the board with a dab
of icing as well.

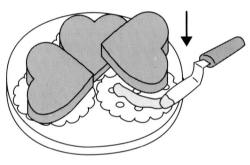

Using the pale green icing and a metal
spatula, cover tops and sides of cakes.
Place stem pattern in place on board
and trace around it with a pencil.
Remove pattern.

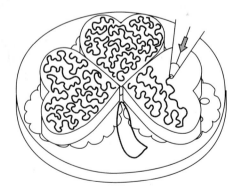

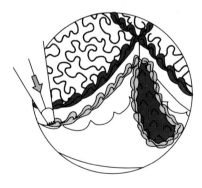

Cut 1 in (2.5cm) off the end of a large
parchment cone and drop coupler
inside. Attach tip #2 and half fill the
cone with dark green Buttercream
Icing. Completely fill in the top of the
heart cakes with cornelli lace (p16).

Using the same cone of icing, attach
tip #16 and make plain shells around
top border on cakes. Fill in shamrock
stem with green icing stars (p17) using
same tip. Cut ½ in (1.3cm) off the tip
of the other parchment cone, drop in

tip #18 and half fill the cone with pale
green icing to make the shell border
around the bottom of cake, as shown.
Outline the shamrock stem with shells
as well.

Bride and Bridesmaids

INGREDIENTS (Bride)		
1	2-layer cake mix or Angel Food Cake (p8)	1
3 cups	Buttercream Icing (p12)	750ml

Bride

EQUIPMENT

1 doll pan (Dolly Varden tin)

10-in (25.4-cm)-round cake plate or
  covered board (p10)

1 large parchment (greaseproof paper) cone

small metal spatula

parchment paper sheet

1 doll pick

tips #16, #104, #18

coupler

9 in (23cm) length of white nylon tulle

needle and white thread

Note If you use tip #18 you will not need a coupler, but you will have to change parchment cones for each different color you use. With tip #18 you will make zigzags instead of ruffles on bride's skirt.

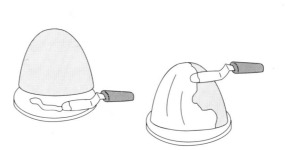

Prepare the cake mix according to the instructions on the cake-mix package or use the Angel Food Cake recipe. Place batter in prepared doll pan (p9). Bake at 350°F (180°C) (gas or electric) for 55 to 60 minutes or until cake tests done (p9). Remove the center core from pan and allow the cake to stand 7 to 10 minutes, then carefully invert onto a cake rack to cool. Cool angel cake as directed in recipe.

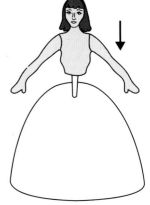

Adhere cake to cake board with a dab of icing. Using a metal spatula, ice the cake with white icing. Use parchment paper to smooth the icing (p15).

Push the doll pick into the cake. Build up the waist with icing around the pick.

Cut 1 in (2.5cm) off the end of the parchment cone, insert coupler, add tip #16, and half fill cone with white icing. Pipe out stars to cover bodice and sleeves. Build up stars for a puffed sleeve effect. Add stars randomly to bride's skirt. Change to tip #104 and

starting at the edge, at the base of the skirt, make 2 rows of ruffles (p16). Change back to tip #16. Just above the 2 rows of ruffles continue making stars with tip #16.

Gather the 9 in (23cm) white tulle along 1 edge with a needle and thread

to fit the doll's head. Bind thread. Attach to the doll's head with a mound of white Buttercream Icing. Pipe icing stars around the mound with tip #16 or #18. This is the bridal head piece.

Bridesmaids are described on p50.

Bridesmaids

EQUIPMENT

1 petite doll pan
3 – 5-in (12.7-cm)-round covered boards (p10)
3 petite doll picks
3 large parchment cones
tips #104, #16 (or use #18)
3 couplers
paste colors: teal blue, violet, pink
toothpicks
ruler
parchment (greaseproof) paper
small metal spatula

Note Tip #18 may be used instead of
#16 and #104. You will not need the
couplers. Tip #104 will make zigzags
instead of ruffles.

INGREDIENTS (Bridesmaids)		
1	1-layer cake mix	1
Buttercream Icing (p12)		
1 cup	teal blue	250ml
1 cup	violet	250ml
1 cup	pink	250ml

Prepare cake mix according to the
instructions on the cake-mix package.
Prepare a petite doll pan (p9). Fill 3
holes each ⅔ full. Bake at 350°F (180°C)
(gas or electric) for 20 to 25 minutes or
until mini cakes test done (p9). Allow
cakes to stand in pans for 5 minutes,
then carefully invert them onto a cake
rack to cool.

Use icing to secure cakes to round
boards. With a metal spatula, ice and
smooth front area of the first cake with
teal blue colored icing, as shown. Allow
to dry. Smooth with parchment.

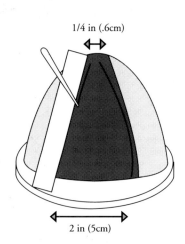

With a ruler and toothpick, mark an
elongated "V" on the iced area
measuring 2 in (5cm) across at the
bottom, tapering gradually to ¼ in
(.6cm) at the waist. Push a doll pick
into the cake and fill in the waist
area with a little icing.

Cut 1 in (2.5cm) off the end of a large
parchment cone, insert a coupler, attach
star tip #16. Fill the cone with teal
blue Buttercream Icing. Cover the
bodice, back, waist, and sides of the
skirt with stars.

Change to tip #104 and edge the base
of the skirt with 2 rows of ruffles (p16).
If you use tip #18 in place of #104,
make zigzags at base of skirt. Using
the same technique, decorate the other
2 dolls, 1 with violet icing, 1 with pink
icing.

School Bus

EQUIPMENT

1 – 10 in (25.4cm) loaf pan
1 – 16 in x 8 in (40.6cm x 20cm) covered
  cake board (p10)
ruler
serrated knife
small metal spatula
palette knife
3 medium parchment (greaseproof paper) cones
tip #16
paste colors: yellow, black
toothpicks

INGREDIENTS		
1	2-layer cake mix	1
	Buttercream Icing (p12)	
2 ½ cups	golden yellow	625ml
½ cup	white	125ml
½ cup	black	125ml
3	ice cream wafers each 2 ½ in (6.4cm) long	3
½ cup	clear piping gel	125ml
4	round flat vanilla wafers or cookies	4
	Smarties or M&M's	
2	red	2
6	yellow	6

Prepare the cake mix according to the instructions on the cake-mix package. Prepare the loaf pan (p9). Bake at 325°F (160°C electric or 180°C gas) for 45 minutes or until cake tests done (p9). Allow cake to cool in pan 5 to 7 minutes, then invert cake onto a rack. When completely cooled, wrap loaf and freeze.

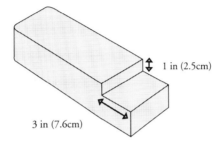

To make front of bus cut a 3 in (7.6cm) slice across the frozen loaf and down 1 in (2.5cm), as shown. Remove this piece of cake and save for hood of cab engine.

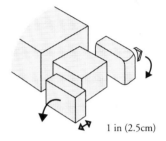

Cut 1 in (2.5cm) down on both sides of the front of the cab, as shown, and remove sides from cake and save for fenders. Round outside top edges with a serrated knife.

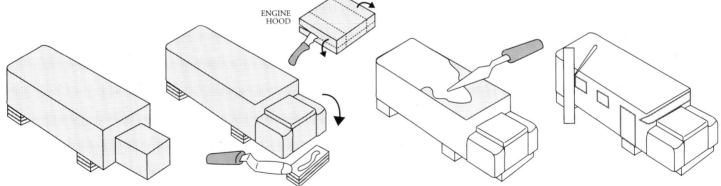

Using the golden yellow icing, attach 2 ice-cream wafers to the board to fit under the rear portion of the bus, positioning 1 wafer at each end, as shown. Using golden yellow icing attach the cut loaf to the wafers.

Attach the rounded fenders to front of cab engine with icing. Elevate the cab end section with ice-cream wafer, cut to fit. Use the 3 in (7.6cm) slice from the top of the loaf for the bus hood. Cut it in half, as shown, and trim to fit the front middle section over engine, *(see photo of uniced cake p52).* Attach the bus hood with the yellow icing.

Thin the remaining golden yellow icing with 2 tsp (10ml) of water and proceed to ice the entire bus using a palette knife. When icing is dry use a small ruler and toothpick to measure 3 individual windows 3½ in (9cm) square on both sides of the bus. On the left side of the bus mark another window. On the right side mark the bus door 2¼ in x 3¼ in (5.7cm x 8.3cm). Mark the front window of the bus ¾ in (2cm) high and extend it across the front to each side, forming a triangle window shape, as shown.

School Bus continued on p52.

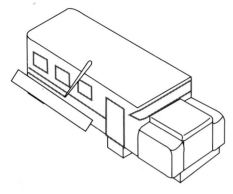

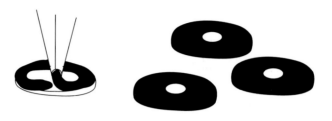

Mark with toothpick 2 – 5 in (13cm) lines ¼ in (.6cm) wide under the bus windows.

Color ½ cup (125ml) of white icing with black paste color. Use a medium

parchment cone, cut ½ in (1.3cm) off the end and drop in tip #16. Half fill cone with the black icing. Hold the cone of icing slightly above a flat cookie at a 90° angle. Squeeze the cone moving the tip in a clockwise circular

direction, as shown, until the cookie wheel is completely covered. Stop the pressure and pull the tip away from the cookie. Attach a yellow candy to the center of cookie. Make 4. Allow to dry. These are the wheels.

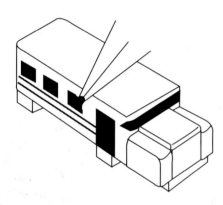

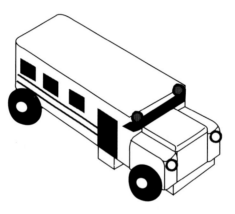

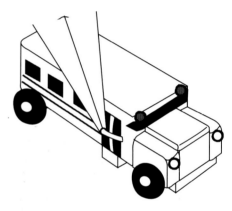

Color the clear piping gel with black paste color. Cut the end off a medium parchment cone to a size 2 hole (p14) and add black gel. Using a zigzag motion, fill in all outlined windows and bus door with the black gel. Fill in

the lines under the windows with black gel. Attach the 4 vanilla cookie wheels to the bus with icing. Attach the 2 red candies to the top of the front window. Add 2 yellow candies at front lower portion of bus cab for headlights.

Add 1 tbs (15ml) of yellow icing to a parchment cone. Cut the end off the cone to a size 4 hole (p14) and pipe in the yellow lines on the bus door, as shown.

UNICED CAKE PARTS

Hockey Sweater

	INGREDIENTS	
1	2-layer cake mix or Never-Fail Chocolate Cake (p8)	1
	Buttercream Icing (p12)	
3 cups	royal blue	750ml
¼ cup	white	50ml
¼ cup	yellow	50ml
2 tsp	clear gel	10ml
3 tsp	red gel	15ml
2 tsp	black gel	10ml
1 tsp	brown gel	5ml
3 tsp	yellow gel	15ml
1 tsp	blue gel	5ml

EQUIPMENT

1 – 9 in x 13 in (22.9cm x 33cm) cake pan
1 – 14-in (35.6-cm)-square covered cake board
baking strips
small metal spatula
hockey player pattern (p93)
parchment paper sheet
tape
non-toxic black marker
toothpicks
7 parchment (greaseproof paper) cones:
   1 large, 6 small
tip #48
paste colors: red, black, brown, yellow, blue
wax paper

Prepare the cake mix according to the instructions on the cake-mix package or use the Never-Fail Chocolate Cake recipe. Prepare the baking pan (p9). Add the cake mixture and wrap pan with baking strips (p9). Bake in a 350°F (180°C) (gas or electric) oven for 25 to 30 minutes or until cake tests done (p9). Remove baking strips. Allow cake to

cool in pan 5 to 7 minutes, then carefully invert cake onto a cake rack to cool completely. Wrap cake and freeze. Cut and remove a 1-in (2.5-cm)-deep half circle, as shown, from the top of the cake for the neck. Cut a 2 in (5cm) strip from the bottom of the cake and cut this strip in half on an angle, as

shown. Place these 2 strips at the top of the cake for the sleeves. Assemble all pieces on the cake board, secure to board, and join parts with icing. Using a small metal spatula and royal blue icing, cover the cake completely. Allow icing to dry. Smooth with parchment paper (p15).

Tape wax paper over hockey pattern and trace with a black non-toxic marker. Cut out. Center the pattern on the cake facing left and trace the outline only with a toothpick. Remove the pattern and ice the entire hockey figure on cake with thinned (p15) white icing using a metal spatula. When dry, smooth with parchment. While the white icing is drying, color

the gel, as specified above. Add black gel to a small parchment cone and cut the end off to a size 1 hole (p14).

Invert wax paper pattern. Using the black gel and squeezing out a continuous line, quickly go over the lines of the hockey picture. *Note: Gel should not dry.* Lift wax paper and invert to fit white icing figure on cake.

Lightly rub gel lines with a toothpick. Lift wax paper off cake and discard pattern.

Cut the black gel cone to a size 2 hole (p14) and re-outline the hockey figure with the black gel. Fill the other small parchment cones with the other colored gel portions and cut cone ends to size 2 holes (p14), as you use them.

Follow the photograph illustration and fill in the hockey player with the different colors. Move cones back and forth in zigzag motions to fill in each area. Make wavy lines with black gel cone under picture, as shown.

Cut ½ in (1.3cm) off the end of a large parchment cone, insert tip #48, and add yellow icing. Pipe the neck and sleeves to give a ribbon effect, as shown.

Tabby Cat

INGREDIENTS		
1	2-layer white cake mix	1
	Buttercream Icing (p12)	
3 cups	light brown	750ml
3 tbs	pink	45ml
1 tbs	dark brown	15ml
1 tbs	white	15ml
6	3 in (7.6cm) pieces thin uncooked spaghetti	6
1	red Smarties or M&M's	1

EQUIPMENT

1 doll pan (Dolly Varden tin)
1 – 10-in (25.4-cm)-round cake stand
small metal spatula
parchment paper
4 parchment (greaseproof paper) cones:
   1 large, 3 medium
coupler
tips #3, #6, #12, #233
paste colors: pink, brown
toothpicks
no.3 art brush

Prepare the cake mix according to the instructions on the cake-mix package. Prepare the baking pan (p9). Add the cake mixture and bake at 350°F (180°C) (gas or electric) for 50 to 60 minutes or until cake tests done (p9). Allow cake to cool in pan 5 to 7 minutes. Remove baking core from doll pan, then carefully invert onto a cake rack to cool completely.

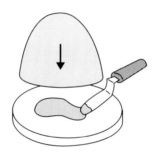

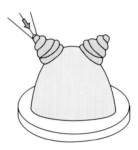

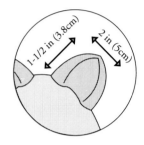

Place cooled cake on the cake stand and secure it to the stand with a dab of icing. Cut 1 in (2.5cm) off the end of a large parchment cone, insert coupler, and attach tip #12. Half fill cone with light brown icing and pipe cat's ears.

Ears should measure 1½ in (3.8cm) high and 2 in (5cm) at the widest or center part of the ears. Using another parchment cone, cut off ½ in (1.3cm) and drop in tip #12. Add pink icing and pipe inside of cat's ears.

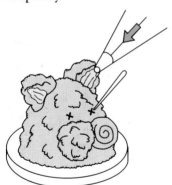

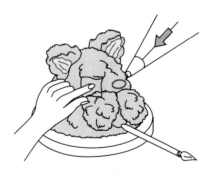

Mark the eyes with a toothpick, and build up mounds of light brown icing under the eyes for cheeks and snout. Change to tip #233 and squeeze out light brown icing strands along the head to completely cover the cake. This will give the effect of fur or hair.

Smooth out the eye section of the icing with parchment paper. Change

to tip #3, and outline the eye with light brown icing. Using the end of the art brush, hollow out a mouth under the cheeks and outline this with tip #3 and light brown icing.

Cut off ½ in (1.3cm) from the end of a medium parchment cone and drop in tip #6. Add dark brown icing to the cone and squeeze out dots for the

center of the eyes. Add a white icing dot to eye for highlight (see photograph). Fill in the nose and outline the cheeks, as shown. Add a red flat candy for the tongue. Cut off ½ in (1.3cm) from end of a medium parchment cone and add white icing. Break spaghetti into pieces 3 in (7.6cm) long. Make spaghetti whiskers (p21) using white icing and add to cheek area.

Easter Basket

INGREDIENTS		
1	2-layer cake mix	1
2 cups	Buttercream Icing (p12)	500ml
1½ cups	long shredded coconut	125g
12	speckled jelly eggs	12
8	pastel-colored chocolate wafers	8

EQUIPMENT

1 – 8-in (20-cm)-round cake pan
   3 in (7.6cm) deep
baking strips
1 – 10-in (25.4-cm)-round
   covered cake board (p10)
small metal spatula
1 large parchment (greaseproof paper) cone
tips #46, #18
coupler
powder color: green
1 plastic bunny mold
2 white chenille stems

Prepare the cake mix according to the instructions on the cake-mix package. Prepare the round cake pan (p9). Add cake mixture, and wrap the pan with baking strips (p9). Bake at 350°F (180°C) (gas or electric) for 30 to 35 minutes or until cake tests done (p9). Remove baking strips and cool the cake on a wire rack for 5 to 7 minutes. Invert cake onto the wire rack and cool completely.

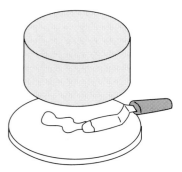

Put dabs of icing onto the covered cake board and position the cooled cake onto the board, flat side up. Thin ½ of white icing with 1 tbs (15ml) of water and apply a thin coat of icing to the cake using a small metal spatula.

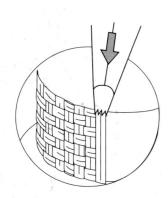

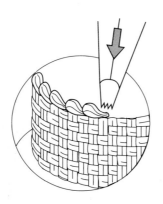

Cut 1 in (2.5cm) off the end of the parchment cone and insert the coupler and attach tip #46. Add some of remaining white icing to cone. Cover sides of cake using the basket weave pattern (p17).

Using the same cone, change to tip #18 and complete a large rope border (p16) around the top of the cake.

Color the shredded coconut green (p22) and sprinkle on top of cake to make the "grass." To make chocolate bunnies, spoon melted wafers (p22) into bunny molds. Tap mold on counter to level wafers and release any air bubbles. Place mold in the refrigerator for 5 or 10 minutes, or until set. Remove from the refrigerator and invert onto counter. Add the

bunnies and speckled eggs to the top of the cake using some Buttercream Icing to hold them in place.

Twist chenille stem ends together, as shown, making a handle. Secure handle to top of cake, as shown. Arrange some colored coconut and eggs around the cake on the cake board and secure with icing (see photograph).

Halloween Novelties

EQUIPMENT
5 small parchment (greaseproof paper) cones:
  3 large, 1 medium, 1 small
tips #17, #14, #16, #4, #104, #1, #3
  #2, #74, #352
2 couplers
paste colors: black, orange, green
scissors

INGREDIENTS		
12	flat cookies 2½ in (6.5cm) in diameter	12
3	miniature marshmallows	3
13	regular or large marshmallows	13
	Buttercream Icing (p12)	
1 cup	black	250ml
1 cup	white	250ml
1 cup	orange	250ml
½ cup	green	125ml
1 tsp	red piping gel	5ml
	sugar add-on eyes (optional)	

Pumpkin

Put a dab of icing on 1 flat surface of a large marshmallow and adhere to a flat cookie. Cut ½ in (1.3cm) off the end of 1 large parchment cone, drop in tip #74, and half fill with orange icing. Pipe a ring around the center of the marshmallow, as shown.

Starting at the top of the marshmallow, pipe icing lines from top to bottom until the marshmallow is completely covered. This resembles pumpkin ridges. Cut 1 in (2.5cm) off the end of a medium parchment cone, insert coupler, add tip #4. Half fill with green icing. Pipe a green stem at the top. Change to tip #352 and pipe green leaves around the bottom of the pumpkin, as shown.

Ghost

   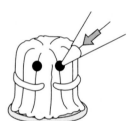

Ice 1½ marshmallows together and ice to a flat cookie. Cut ½ in (1.3cm) off the end of a large parchment cone and insert tip #16. Half fill with white icing. Cover marshmallow with long lines of icing, starting at the top of the marshmallow and extending the lines down the marshmallow and out onto the cookie, as shown. Using the same tip, pipe the arms. Cut 1 in (2.5cm) off the end of another large parchment cone, insert coupler, add tip #2 and half fill cone with black icing. Make eyes.

Cat

Cut 1 large marshmallow with scissors, as shown. Ice a small marshmallow on top. Ice the flat bottom of the angled marshmallow on the flat cookie. Using cone of black icing and tip #17 make black icing stars to cover marshmallow. Use the same tip to pipe the front legs, hind legs, and tail, as shown. Change to tip #3 and add the ears. Change to tip #1 and add the whiskers. Add sugar candy eyes and nose.

60

Witch

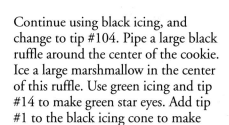

Continue using black icing, and change to tip #104. Pipe a large black ruffle around the center of the cookie. Ice a large marshmallow in the center of this ruffle. Use green icing and tip #14 to make green star eyes. Add tip #1 to the black icing cone to make black pupils and pipe eyebrows. Pipe

a long nose with tip #14 and green icing. Add red gel to a small parchment cone. Cut the end off the cone to a size 1 hole (p14) and pipe the mouth. Change the tip on the black icing cone to tip #12 and pipe a tall hat by holding the bag at a 90° angle and decreasing the pressure as you lift the

tip straight up to form a dome or peaked hat.

Change to tip #104 on the black icing cone and pipe a brim on the hat, making sure the wide end of the tip is touching the marshmallow. Complete the hair on the marshmallow using tip #16 and the orange icing cone.

Autumn Harvest

INGREDIENTS		
1	2-layer cake mix	1
1	ice-cream cone	1
Buttercream Icing (p12)		
2 cups	white	500ml
1 cup	golden yellow	250ml
¾ cup	tan	175ml
1 cup	green	250ml
Marzipan fruits and vegetables *(recipe included p64)*		

EQUIPMENT

1 – 9 in x 13 in (22.9cm x 33cm) cake pan
1 – 10 in x 14 in (25.4cm x 35.6cm) covered
  cake board (p10)
baking strips
small metal spatula
parchment paper
sharp knife
3 large parchment (greaseproof paper) cones
tips #8, #46, #18, #16, #4
2 couplers
paste colors: golden yellow, tan, green
toothpicks
rolling pin
pastry brush

Prepare the cake mix according to the instructions on the cake-mix package. Prepare the baking pan (p9). Add cake mixture and wrap the pan with baking strips (p9). Bake at 350°F (180°C) (gas or electric) for 30 to 35 minutes or until cake tests done (p9). Remove baking strips and allow cake to stand in pan 5 to 7 minutes. Invert the cake onto a large cake rack and cool completely.

Place cake on prepared cake board and secure with icing. Completely cover with white Buttercream Icing using small metal spatula. Smooth cake

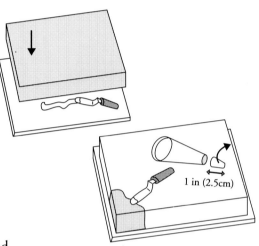

surface (p15). Cut 1 in (2.5cm) off the end of the ice-cream cone and discard. Position cone on the cake, as shown.

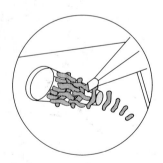
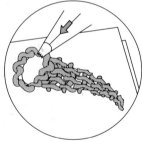

Cut 1 in (2.5cm) off the end of a large parchment cone and drop in coupler. Attach tip #8 and half fill the parchment cone with tan icing. Make vertical lines on the ice-cream cone. Change to tip #46 and make horizontal lines on the ice-cream cone, as shown. Change to tip #18 and add a rope border (p16) around the opening of

the ice-cream cone to complete the cornucopia.

Cut 1 in (2.5cm) off the end of a large parchment cone. Drop in coupler and half fill parchment cone with green icing. Add tip #16 and make a zigzag border (p16) around the top of the cake. Change tip to #4. Draw the message on top of the cake with a

toothpick, then trace this with tip #4 and the green icing.

Cut ½ in (1.3cm) off the end of a large parchment cone. Insert tip #18 and add golden yellow icing. Complete shell border (p16) at bottom of the cake.

Arrange marzipan fruits and vegetables inside and around the cornucopia, as shown.

Marzipan Fruits & Vegetables on p64.

Marzipan Fruits & Vegetables

INGREDIENTS		
1 lb	almond paste	.5kg
5 tbs	glucose	75ml
2 cups	icing sugar	270g
½ cup	corn syrup	125ml

EQUIPMENT

paste colors: orange, red, green, yellow

whole cloves for stems

oil flavoring (optional)

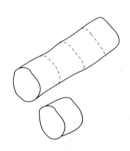  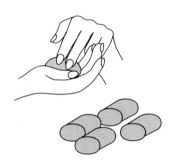 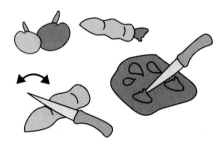

Warm the glucose for 20 seconds in microwave and stir it into the almond paste. Add icing sugar and blend. Knead the mixture until the marzipan has a consistency of pie dough.

Divide the dough into 5 portions and color each portion using paste colors and toothpicks of orange, red, green, and yellow respectively. Do not color one of the portions. You may add oil flavoring at the same time that you knead the colors. Oil flavoring makes this recipe taste delicious. Add lime or apple oil flavoring to the green, strawberry flavoring to the red, orange flavoring to the orange, and lemon flavoring to the yellow.

Sprinkle icing sugar on the counter and roll the marzipan with your hand into a long rope 1 in (2.5cm) thick. Slice rope into pieces the sizes of fruits you want. Shape and roll these pieces into balls or tapered shapes. Apples, pears, bananas, carrots can be created using this technique. Make potatoes from uncolored portion. Use a sharp knife to make grooves in the carrots and a toothpick or wooden skewer to make holes. Add cloves for stems. Roll out green marzipan with rolling pin and cut shaped leaves and strands for carrots, apples, etc. Thin corn syrup with 1 tbs (15ml) water. Heat slightly. Brush on marzipan fruits and vegetables as a glaze.

Fire Truck

EQUIPMENT

1 – 8 in (20cm) loaf pan
baking strips
1 – 18 in x 8 in (45.7cm x 20cm)
   covered cake board (p10)
ruler
serrated knife
small metal spatula
1 large parchment (greaseproof paper) cone
tips #16, #4
coupler
paste colors: red, black
palette knife
4 – 7½ in (19cm) yellow straws
1 empty thread spool
toothpicks
wafer (rice) paper
art brush

INGREDIENTS		
1	2-layer cake mix	1
1	1-layer cake mix	1
Buttercream Icing (p12)		
3 cups	red	750ml
½ cup	grey	125ml
½ cup	black	125ml
1 tbs	clear piping gel	15ml
6	flat cookies or vanilla wafers	6
6	yellow Smarties or M&M's	6
black licorice strings		
8	ice-cream wafers	8
2	bugles	2

This is how cake will be assembled.

Prepare the 2-layer cake mix according to the instructions on the cake-mix package. Prepare the loaf pan (p9). Add cake mixture and wrap the pan with baking strips (p9). Bake at 325°F (160°C electric or 180°C gas) for 45 to 50 minutes or until cake tests done

(p9). Allow to stand on a wire rack for 5 to 7 minutes. Remove baking strips. Invert loaf onto cake rack to cool completely. Wash and dry pan. Prepare as

before. Prepare the 1-layer cake mix in the same way and bake in the same loaf pan 20 to 25 minutes or until done. Invert on wire rack, as above.

When loaves are completely cooled, wrap and freeze. Use the largest loaf for the rear of the fire truck. Slice off and discard one end to make flat surface.

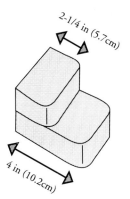

Cut remaining loaf into truck parts as follows:

    1 truck cab   4 in (10.2cm) long
    1 cab top   2¼ in (5.7cm) long

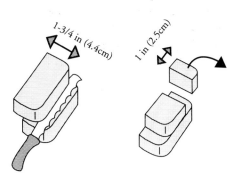

Cut remaining 1¾ in (4.4cm) piece in half, as shown. Use one piece for bottom deep step. Cut 1 in (2.5cm) off the side of second half and place over deep step.

Fire Truck continued on p66.

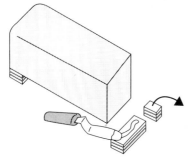

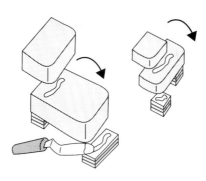

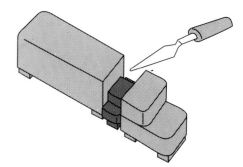

Attach 2 ice-cream wafers one at each end of 8 in (20cm) loaf (truck body). Cut wafers to fit width of truck body. Secure with dab of icing, as shown. Ice truck body with red icing using metal

spatula and smooth (p15). Join pieces of truck cab with dabs of icing. Attach 2 ice-cream wafers under cab, as shown, and secure with dabs of icing. Cut wafers to fit width of cab.

Ice and smooth truck cab with red icing and palette knife. Attach 2 ice-cream wafer pieces under steps. Ice steps with grey icing. Position steps between truck body and cab. Secure with icing.

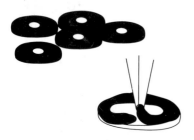

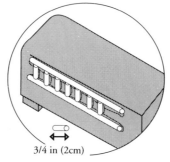

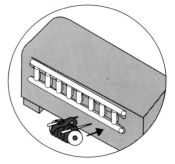

Using a large parchment cone, cut 1 in (2.5cm) off the end, drop in coupler, and add tip #16. Partly fill cone with black icing. Pipe icing on the vanilla cookies or wafers for wheels. Hold the icing cone at a 90° angle with tip slightly above the cookie. Squeeze, moving the tip in a clockwise, circular motion,

as shown, until the cookie wheel is completely covered. Stop pressure and then pull the tip away. Add a yellow flat candy in the center of the cookie. Set wheels aside and allow to dry.

Ice 2 of the straws to the side of fire truck, as shown. Cut the remaining

straws into ¾ in (2cm) rails and place them with icing inside the long straws, as shown. This is the ladder. Repeat for other side.

Wrap licorice string around the empty spool and attach with toothpicks to the side of the fire truck.

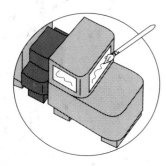

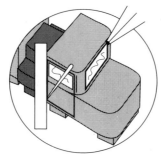

Cut 2 – 1 in (2.5cm) squares of wafer (rice) paper for the side windows and 1 piece 2½ in x 1 in (6.4cm x 2.5cm) for front window. Brush clear piping gel on the rough side of the wafer paper windows and apply to the iced truck. Apply a top coat of gel to the windows for a shiny look.

Draw doors on the truck cab with a toothpick and ruler. Change tip on black icing cone to tip #4 to outline around doors and wafer windows.

Ice the bugles to the top of the cab. Attach yellow Smarties or M&M's

using black icing to the front of the cab for headlights. Change the tip on the black icing cone to tip #16 to zigzag (p16) the front and rear bumpers. Attach wheels to sides of truck, as shown.

Circus Train

This project takes 2 days to complete

EQUIPMENT
4 large parchment (greaseproof paper) cones
tips #3, #16, #18
3 couplers
paste colors: red, yellow
cage car pattern (p93)

	INGREDIENTS	
1 box	graham wafers	1 box
	strings of black licorice	
8	round chocolate-filled cookies	8
	Royal Icing (p12)	
1 cup	red	250ml
1 cup	yellow	250ml
1 cup	white	250ml
	Smarties or M&M's	
4	yellow	4
8	red	8
4	green	4
26	assorted colors	26
	assorted small candies, lifesavers, ball-type suckers, and candy sticks to fill train cars	
18	flat licorice disks (for wheels)	18
3	licorice candies (for front of train)	3
17	ice-cream wafers	17
1 pkg	silver dragees	1 pkg

First day

Cut 1 in (2.5cm) off a large parchment cone, insert a coupler, and attach tip #16. The train parts will be iced together using white Royal Icing and this tip. The train will be decorated with red, yellow, and white Royal Icing.

Allow the train and cars to dry overnight when they are put together.

Engine

Ice together (flat sides to flat sides) 6 round chocolate-filled cookies, as shown. This is the engine. To make the cab, stand 4 full-size graham wafers upright like a box and ice together, as shown. (A full-size graham wafer measures 4¾ in or 12cm long). Cut 3 graham wafers to 3 in (7.6cm) long, stack them, and ice them together for engine platform.

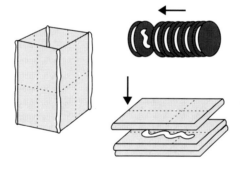

Position the platform in front of the cab with Royal Icing. Place the engine of chocolate cookies on top of platform, and hold in place with icing, as shown. Attach flat licorice candy pieces 1 in x

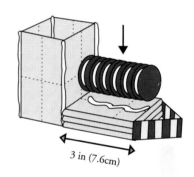

3 in (7.6cm)

3 in (2.5cm x 7.6cm) decorated with yellow candy stripes to front of engine at an angle, as shown. This is the cow catcher.

Coal Car

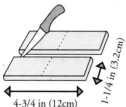

4-3/4 in (12cm)

1-1/4 in (3.2cm)

Cut 1 full-size wafer in half lengthwise. These are car sides, each 1¼ in (3.2cm) high and 4¾ in (12cm) long. Make car ends by cutting a full-size graham wafer

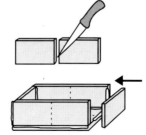

in half, then cut in half again. Make the bottom of car with 1 full-size graham wafer. Hold together with icing. Cut ice-cream wafers to 3 in

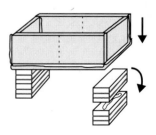

(7.5cm) long. Stack 2 and ice together and adhere with icing to the bottom of one end of the car, as shown. Repeat for other end.

Circus Train continued on p70.

Circus Train *continued*

Cage Car

Use 2 full-size graham wafers 4¾ in (12cm) long for the sides. Cut 1 full-size wafer in half for the car ends. Line bottoms with 1 full-size wafer. Hold together with icing. Cut 12 licorice strings each 2¼ in (5.7cm) long and attach to side of car with icing. Place

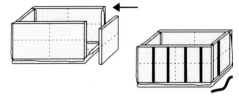

4 per side and 2 at each end, as shown. Cut 1 full-size wafer in half. Then, using pattern, cut 1 curved top from each half. Ice these curved wafers to

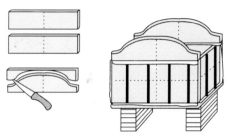

the top sides of the cage car. Elevate the car with stacked ice-cream wafers, as for coal car.

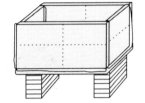

Circus Car

Use 2 full-size wafers for each side and 1 wafer cut in half for the ends of the circus car. Line the bottom with 1 full-size wafer. Put together with icing. Cut and stack ice-cream wafers to elevate car, as for coal car.

Caboose

Use full-size graham wafer for each side and cut off approximately 1 in (2.5cm) from end. Line bottom with 1 wafer cut to same size as sides. Use a half graham wafer for each end. Put

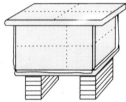

together with icing. Use 1 full-size wafer for the top of the caboose (ends will hang over). Elevate the caboose with stacked ice-cream wafers, as for coal car.

Second day

The train will be decorated with red, yellow, and white Royal Icing. Cut 1 in (2.5cm) off the end of a large parchment cone and drop in a coupler. Attach tip #18 and half fill cone with white icing. Cut 1 in (2.5cm) off the end of another large parchment cone.

Drop in coupler and attach tip #16. Half fill with yellow icing. This is used to complete zigzags (p16), stars, and shell borders (p16) that cover the seams and edges on cars. Cut 1 in (2.5cm) off the end of another large parchment cone, drop in coupler, and attach tip #3. Half fill cone with red icing.

Ice the flat licorice candies to the ice-cream wafers at bottom of cars for the wheels. Ice 2 licorice candies to front of engine for wheels. Add an icing star with yellow icing cone and tip #16 to the center of each wheel and dot with a silver dragee.

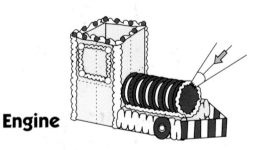

Engine

Outline a window on each side of engine cab with zigzag border (p16) using tip #16 and yellow icing. Add a flat red candy immediately to the 4 corners of each window. Using white icing and tip #18, complete white zigzag borders (p16) to cover all edges. Make shells on top edge of cab using same tip. Immediately decorate with colored Smarties or M&M's. Use the

same tip to zigzag a border around the front of the engine and larger zigzags to line along bottom of engine. Ice a lifesaver to the front of the engine and use a green candy for the headlight. Ice to center of lifesaver. Stack 2 lifesavers, ice together, and attach to engine with white icing for smoke stack. Place red ball candy on top and attach with white icing. Using red icing, attach tip

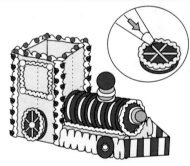

#16 and make star decoration on white border edges, as shown. Decorate 2 round chocolate cookies for large wheels. Using yellow icing cone, attach tip #3 and pipe spokes for the wheels. Change to tip #16 and make yellow zigzags for wheel rims. Place yellow Smarties or M&M's for hub in the centers of each wheel. Attach a wheel to each side of engine cab with a dab of icing.

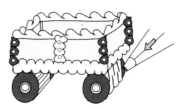

Coal Car

With yellow icing and tip #16, make a zigzag border around the bottom edges of the coal car. Using the same tip, make icing shells on the top edges of the car. Make flat stars with yellow

icing to cover center seams and place 3 silver dragees on each side of car. Use red icing and tip #16. Make 3 red stars at each end of car. Attach 3 silver dragees immediately.

Use yellow icing and attach tip #16. Make large zigzag border to cover ice-cream wafers at ends of car, as shown.

Cage Car

Use red icing and tip #16 and make shell borders all around top and bottom of curved pieces at top of car and use icing stars (same tip) to fill in backs of curved pieces. Place silver dragees along red bottom edge of each curved

piece. Use yellow icing and tip #16 and make 2 rows of icing stars at each end of cage car and 1 row along the bottom of each side, and to cover seam on curved top. Add silver dragees, as shown, and adhere colored candies with icing,

as shown. With same tip make a row of yellow shells at top and bottom ends of car. Make a yellow zigzag border to cover ice-cream wafers showing at ends of car.

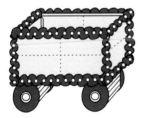

Circus Car

Using red icing and tip #16 make a zigzag border around all edges of circus car. Attach silver dragees immediately.

Using yellow icing and tip #16 make large zigzags to cover ice-cream wafers showing at ends of car. Attach animal

crackers to sides of car with a dab of icing. Use yellow icing and tip #3 to outline around animals.

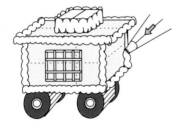
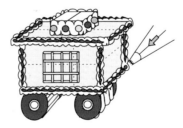
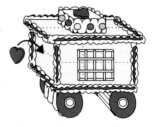

Caboose

Cut 1 ice-cream wafer in half and ice the 2 halves, side by side, to the roof of the caboose. Using white icing and tip #3, pipe a window on each side of the car. Change to tip #18 and make

small zigzags around all edges and around edges of ice-cream wafers. Place colored Smarties or M&M's around wafers. Using red icing and tip #16 make small shells over the white zigzags

on the caboose. Place a red heart candy at back of caboose with a dab of icing. Fill cars with assorted candies.

71

Airplane

INGREDIENTS		
2	2-layer cake mixes	2
	Buttercream Icing (p12)	
4½ cups	white	1.2L
½ cup	red	125ml
½ cup	royal blue	125ml
½ cup	yellow	125ml
¼ cup	clear piping gel	50ml

EQUIPMENT

1 – 11 in x 15 in (27.9cm x 38.1cm) cake pan

1 – 20-in (50.8-cm)-round covered
 cake board (p10)

baking strips

serrated knife

small metal spatula

4 parchment (greaseproof paper) cones:
 1 large, 3 medium

tips #18, #4

4 couplers

paste colors: red, royal blue, yellow

wafer (rice) paper

no.3 art brush

airplane, windows, and bull's-eye patterns
 (p93)

Prepare the cake mixes according to the instructions on the cake-mix packages. Prepare the baking pan (p9). Add cake mixture and wrap the pan with baking strips (p9). Bake at 350°F (180°C) (gas or electric) for 35 to 40 minutes or until cake tests done (p9). Remove strips. Allow the cake to stand 5 to 7 minutes, then invert onto a cake rack to cool. Wrap and freeze cake.

Cut the airplane parts from the frozen cake according to pattern.

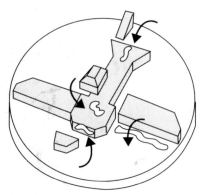

Using a small amount of thinned white Buttercream Icing, ice the pieces together and ice to covered cake board. Make airplane windows from the wafer (rice) paper, using pattern. Cut out.

Brush clear gel on the rough side of the wafer paper windows and attach to plane. When attached, brush a coat of clear gel on top of wafer paper.

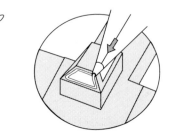

Cut 1 in (2.5çm) off the end of a large parchment cone and insert a coupler and attach tip #4. Put half the white icing in cone. Outline the windows with heavy white line.

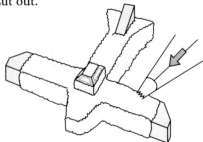

Change to tip #18. Cover plane with icing stars. Leave a 3 in (7.6cm) portion on end of each wing for the colored stripes.

Cut 1 in (2.5cm) off the end of

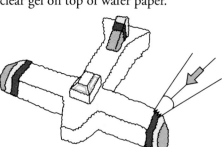

1 medium parchment cone and insert coupler and add tip #18. Fill the cone with red icing and fill in red icing stars to make a 1 in (2.5cm) stripe on wing tips and tail, as shown. Do the same procedure for a yellow stripe and a blue stripe.

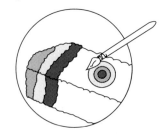

Trace the bull's-eye onto wafer paper and cut out. Apply gel to bull's-eye. Use art brush to apply red, yellow, and blue paste colors respectively, and paint the wafer paper bull's-eye, as shown. Attach to plane with gel.

Dog

EQUIPMENT

1 doll pan (Dolly Varden tin)
1 – 10-in (25.4-cm)-round covered
  cake board (p10)
small metal spatula
1 – 12 in (30.5cm) plastic-lined cloth bag
1 small parchment (greaseproof paper) cone
tips #10, #22
coupler
toothpicks
palette knife
no.3 art brush
dog ear pattern (p93)
bristol board

INGREDIENTS		
1	2-layer white cake mix	1
6 cups	No-Cook Marshmallow Frosting (p13)	1.5L
2 tbs	black Royal Icing (p12), or use black gel	25ml
2	marshmallows	2
1	red Smarties or M&M's	1

Prepare the cake mix according to the instructions on the cake-mix package. Prepare the doll pan (p9). Add cake mixture and bake at 350°F (180°C) (gas or electric) for 55 to 60 minutes or until cake tests done (p9). Remove from oven and allow cake to cool in the pan for 5 to 7 minutes. Remove baking core from doll pan, then turn cake onto a wire rack to cool.

Place cooled cake on cake board and secure to board with a dab of icing. Using the plastic-lined cloth bag, cut off 1 in (2.5cm), insert coupler, and attach tip #22. Half fill with Marshmallow Icing.

Squeeze and pull out long hair-like stars for fur. Completely cover the top and back of the cake. Place 2 marshmallows for cheeks at the front of the cake and position them with toothpicks.

Change tip to #10 and, keeping the tip buried in the icing, fill out the front of the face. Shape the cheeks and forehead using the palette knife. Use an art brush to shape the mouth. Insert a flat red candy for the tongue.

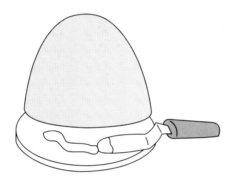

Using the same tip, pull hair-like strands down over the forehead and around the cheeks. Pipe large eyebrows with the same tip. Add the black Royal Icing or black gel to a small parchment cone. Cut the end off the cone to a size 5 hole (p14) and pipe eyes and nose.

Trace the dog's ear pattern onto bristol board, cut out, and attach to the top of the cake. Cover the ears with hair-like strands of icing using the Marshmallow Icing and tip #22.

Cross

EQUIPMENT

1 – 9 in x 13 in (22.9cm x 33cm) cake pan
baking strips
1 – 14-in (35.6-cm)-square covered
   cake board (p10)
small metal spatula
8 parchment (greaseproof paper) cones:
   2 large, 6 small
tips #2, #16, #352
coupler
paste colors: black, yellow, blue, red, green
toothpicks
yellow or white artificial stamens
cross and window patterns (p94)

INGREDIENTS		
Lilies: Royal Icing (p12)		
1 cup	white	250ml
1 tbs	yellow	15ml
1	2-layer cake mix	1
Cooked Whipped Icing (p12)		
2 cups	white	500ml
½ cup	green	125ml
1½ cups	yellow	375ml
½ cup	clear piping gel	125ml
1 tbs (15ml) each yellow, blue, red, white, black		

Prepare the lilies the day before you will use them (p20). You will need a lily nail set, 2-in (5-cm) -foil squares, and extra parchment cones. Make Royal Icing for lilies.

Prepare the cake mix according to the instructions on the cake-mix package. Prepare the baking pan (p9). Add cake mixture and wrap pan with baking strips (p9). Bake at 350°F (180°C) (gas or electric) for 30 to 35 minutes or until cake tests done (p9). Remove strips. Allow the cake to cool in the pan for 5 to 7 minutes then invert cake on a rack to cool completely.

Cut the cake following the pattern, and adhere the pieces to the cake board with a dab of icing. Cover the cake with white Cooked Whipped Icing using a small metal spatula. Smooth icing with spatula.

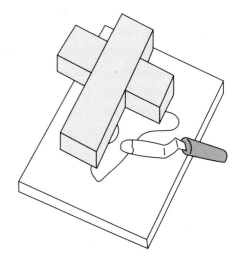

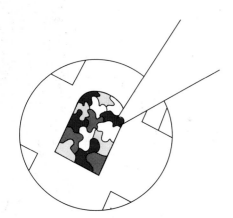

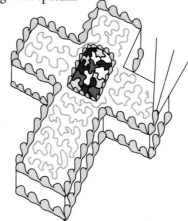

Trace a stained glass window pattern on cake with a toothpick. Cut the end off a small parchment cone to a size 2 hole (p14), and half fill the cone with black gel. Outline the window and the inside lines to resemble the joins of stained glass. Put each color of gel (as above) in separate small parchment cones. Cut cone ends to size 3 hole (p14). Using a back and forth motion

pipe in window sections with the different colored gels.

Cut 1 in (2.5cm) off the end of a large parchment cone. Drop in a coupler, add tip #2 and add yellow Cooked Whipped Icing. Cover top of cake with cornelli lace (p16).

Make shell borders (p16) around win-

dow and top and bottom edges of cross using tip #16 and same cone of icing.

Arrange lilies around the window and down the front of the cake using the photograph as a placement guide. Cut a large parchment cone to form a leaf pattern (p20) or cut ½ in (1.3cm) off the end of a small parchment cone and insert tip #352. Add green Cooked Whipped Icing and make leaves (p20).

Christmas Place Names

Makes 6 place names

	INGREDIENTS	
12	2¾-in (7-cm)-round flat cookies	12
12	large marshmallows	12
	Buttercream Icing (p12)	
1 cup	red	250ml
1 cup	green	250ml
1 cup	white	250ml
½ cup	yellow	125ml
2 tbs	black piping gel	25ml
12	silver dragees	12
	sugar eyes (optional)	

EQUIPMENT
5 parchment (greaseproof paper) cones:
  4 large, 1 small
tips #16, #3, #17, #352, #18, #4
3 couplers
paste colors: red, green, yellow, black
scissors

Santa

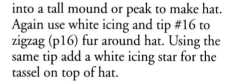

Place 1 large marshmallow on a flat cookie and adhere with a dab of icing. Cut ½ in (1.3cm) off the end of a parchment cone and drop in tip #16. Half fill cone with white icing and pipe eyebrows, mustache, hair, and beard.

Add sugar eyes. Prepare another cone with 1 in (2.5cm) cut end, drop in coupler, add tip #3, and add red icing. Pipe nose and mouth. Change tip on red icing cone to #17 and swirl icing

into a tall mound or peak to make hat. Again use white icing and tip #16 to zigzag (p16) fur around hat. Using the same tip add a white icing star for the tassel on top of hat.

Boot

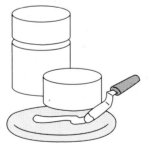

Adhere 1 large marshmallow to a flat cookie with a dab of icing. This is the boot leg. Cut another large marshmallow in half and use one half for the toe or boot's front, as shown. Ice the remaining half to the leg portion, as shown.

Using red icing cone and tip #17, cover the front of boot and bottom half of leg with icing stars (p17). Using white icing cone and tip #16, zigzag (p16) fur at top of boot or top ½ of marshmallow. Pipe white icing fill-in stars across the top of the boot.

Cut 1 in (2.5cm) off the end of another parchment cone, drop in coupler, and add tip #352 or see p20 if you do not have tip #352. Add green icing. Pipe leaves for holly. Add tip #3 to red icing cone to make berries.

Christmas Tree

Adhere 1 large marshmallow to a flat cookie with a dab of icing. Cut another large marshmallow to a point or elongated "V," as shown, and ice to first marshmallow.

Using green icing cone, cover both marshmallows with leaves. For best results, pipe a ring of icing around the base of the marshmallow first. Cover this line with a row of leaves. Repeat

rows of leaves, overlapping each row until marshmallows are covered. Complete top of tree with 90° stand-up leaves. Decorate the tree with silver dragees. *Christmas Place Names continued on p80.*

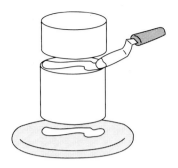

Candle

Use 1½ large marshmallows. Ice the marshmallows together, as shown, and place them on a flat cookie. Adhere with icing. Using the red icing cone and tip #17, pipe large zigzags (p16)

from the top to the bottom of the marshmallows. Fill in top of candle with stars (p17) using red icing cone and tip #17.

Cut ½ in (1.3cm) off the end of another parchment cone and drop in tip #18. Add yellow icing. Add the flame. Pipe stars with tip #16 and white icing cone around the base of candle.

shape marshmallow with scissors

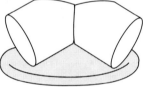

Bells

Cut 2 large marshmallows, as shown. Lay marshmallows at an angle and ice to cookie, as shown. Use yellow icing cone and tip #18 to pipe stars to cover sides of bells. Swirl ends of bells with

tip #16 and white icing cone, as shown. Do this by squeezing the icing cone in a clockwise circular motion until the ends of the bells are completely covered. Using yellow icing cone and

tip #18, add a shell border trim (p16) around the bells. Pipe a figure "8" bow (p17) and clappers using green icing cone and tip #4. Attach an inverted "V" for ties and a dot of icing for a knot.

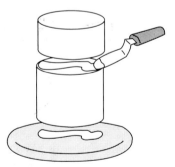

Snowman

Use 1½ large marshmallows. Ice the marshmallows one on top of the other and adhere the bottom marshmallow to a flat cookie with a dab of icing. Use tip #16 and white icing cone to cover entire snowman with icing stars

(p17). Pipe arms as well. Pipe a red hat with tip #17 and red icing cone. To do this, squeeze the cone of icing in a clockwise direction, building up icing to a point. Pipe a red scarf. Cut the end of a small parchment cone to a size 2

hole (p14). Add black piping gel and pipe the mouth, eyes, nose, and buttons on the snowman. Use the same cone of black gel to pipe place names on each marshmallow figure (p21).

Chocolate Ganache

INGREDIENTS		
1	2-layer cake mix or Never-Fail Chocolate Cake (p8)	1
	1 recipe Chocolate Ganache Glaze	
	2 recipes Chocolate Modeling Paste	
	Chocolate Modeling Paste roses and leaves	

EQUIPMENT

1 – 10-in (25.4-cm)-round cake pan
  3 in (7.6cm) deep
baking strips
1 – 12 in (30.5cm) cake plate or
  covered round board
saucepan
sheet of wax or parchment (greaseproof) paper
small metal spatula
sharp paring knife
leaf pattern (p94)
cookie sheet

Prepare 2 recipes of Chocolate Modeling Paste 12 to 24 hours BEFORE using. Use dark chocolate wafers for the first recipe and milk or light chocolate wafers for the second recipe.

Melt the wafers in a large glass measuring cup or bowl in the microwave using DEFROST setting. Warm the glucose in saucepan over low heat and add to the warm melted wafers. Stir thoroughly to blend. DO NOT OVER STIR. This will cause the wafers to separate.

Chocolate Modeling Paste
(1 recipe)

INGREDIENTS		
1 cup or 10 oz melted chocolate wafers (p22)		250ml
½ cup	warmed glucose	125ml

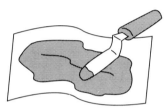 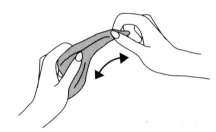

Spread this thick mixture onto a sheet of wax paper or parchment. Cool.

Wrap in plastic and store in a container until ready to use.

To work the modeling paste, knead it with your hands just until it is pliable.

Pull and stretch the paste, fold over, and repeat. If you have warm hands, the paste could become shiny and sticky. If this happens, lay that piece of modeling paste aside and work another piece of the paste while the former piece is cooling.

Chocolate Ganache Glaze

INGREDIENTS		
12 oz	chocolate wafers	375g
1 cup	whipping cream	250ml

Prepare the cake mix according to the instructions on the cake-mix package or make the Never-Fail Chocolate Cake recipe. Prepare the baking pan (p9), add cake mixture, and wrap pan with baking strips (p9). Bake at 350°F (180°C) (gas or electric) for 45 to 55 minutes or until cake tests done (p9). Allow cake to stand 5 to 7 minutes, then invert onto a wire rack to cool completely.

Prepare the Chocolate Ganache Glaze.

Finely chop wafers in a food processor. Scald whipping cream in a saucepan. DO NOT BOIL. Add chopped wafers and stir until smooth. Allow to cool a few minutes. Check thickness for pouring. The cooler the glaze the thicker it will become. Make sure it will pour easily. Always pour the Ganache Glaze onto the center of the cake and allow it to extend towards the edges.

Any leftover glaze can be whipped and used to pipe borders and flowers.

Chocolate Ganache continued on p82.

Chocolate Ganache *continued*

Place the cooled cake on a wire rack that is set on a wax-paper-lined cookie sheet. Pour the glaze onto the center of the cake and down the sides. After the glaze has set, place the cake on the cake plate or round board.

Use some of the prepared Modeling Paste to create the rope-like border around the cake. With your hands roll out 1 long portion of the dark Chocolate Modeling Paste and

 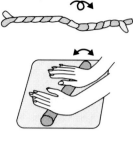 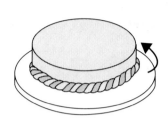

1 long portion of the light Chocolate Modeling Paste to make long coils ½ in (1.3cm) thick and about 28 in (71cm) long. Twist the 2 chocolate

coils together to make a rope and carefully place this rope around the base of the cake. Cut to fit.

To Make Roses

Use the light and dark Chocolate Modeling Paste to create the roses for the top of the cake. As with the icing rose (p18), you must start with a base. The larger the rose, the larger the base. Roll a small piece of Modeling Paste into a ball and shape this ball into a

  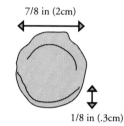

7/8 in (2cm)

1/8 in (.3cm)

dome-shaped base. Petals are formed by flattening small balls of Modeling Paste between your fingers. The bud

and first row of 3 petals should be flattened and shaped to ⅞ in (2cm) diameter and ⅛ in (.3cm) thick.

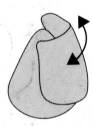 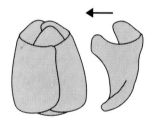 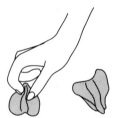 

The first petal is wrapped around the top of the dome-shaped base to form the bud. Three additional petals are pleated and pressed under the bud to form a half rose. Pinch the edges of

the petals to the desired shape.

Flatten and prepare 5 additional petals using the same method. These petals should be about the size of a quarter.

Pleat, pinch, and press the petals under and in between the first row of petals, as shown. Cut off excess base.

Make 3 or 4 large roses and 2 smaller ones (see photograph).

To Make Leaves

Roll out a small amount of Chocolate Modeling Paste using a small roller or rolling pin. Lay the leaf pattern on paste and cut out with a sharp paring knife. Trace the leaf veins using the same paring knife, as shown.

Arrange the roses and leaves on the cake, as shown.

Confirmation

EQUIPMENT

1 – 9 in x 13 in (22.9cm x 33cm) cake pan
1 – 14 in x 18 in (35.6cm x 45.7cm)
  covered cake board
small metal spatula
serrated knife
cake comb
parchment paper
wafer (rice) paper
no.3 art brush
1 medium parchment (greaseproof paper) cone
tip #16
paste colors: yellow, purple, blue,
  black, red, green, brown
paper towel
white plastic lid
non-toxic brown and black markers
wax paper
16 in (40.6cm) yellow ribbon
  1 in (2.5cm) wide
book picture pattern (p94)
verse pattern (p95)

INGREDIENTS		
1	2-layer cake mix	1
	Buttercream Icing (p12)	
1½ cups	white	375ml
3 cups	yellow	750ml
2 tbs	clear piping gel	25ml

Prepare the cake mix according to the instructions on the cake-mix package. Prepare the baking pan (p9). Add cake mixture and wrap the pan with baking strips (p9). Bake at 350°F (180°C) (gas or electric) for 30 to 35 minutes or until cake tests done (p9). Remove baking strips and allow to cool in the pan for 5 to 7 minutes, then carefully invert cake onto a wire rack to cool completely.

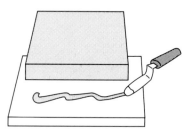

Place cooled cake on cake board and adhere with a dab of icing.

Cut out a 1 in (2.5cm) wedge along the center of the cake in a "V" shape, as shown, for book gutter. Make this cut-out piece into crumbs. Mix 1 cup (250 ml) of yellow Buttercream Icing

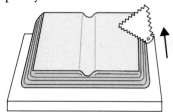

with the cut-out center cake crumbs. Use this mixture to ice the sides and ends of the cake, slanting from top to bottom to give texture to book, as shown. After this has dried, lightly ice with plain yellow Buttercream Icing using metal spatula. Use a cake comb

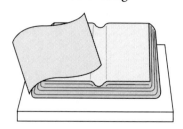

(p15) to create lines for book pages on the yellow icing. Ice the top of the cake with white Buttercream Icing using a metal spatula. Smooth the top of cake using the parchment paper method (p15).

Wafer (rice) paper picture may be traced and painted a few days before baking the cake. With smooth side up, place the wafer paper over the pattern. Use a paper clip to hold the wafer paper on the pattern. Trace the picture with a brown non-toxic pen. Place the completed wafer paper drawing on a piece of wax paper and cover picture with clear gel. Allow to dry 10 to 15 minutes.

Mix paste colors on a large white plastic lid (like an artist's palette). Start with a small toothpick of paste color and add the desired amount of water to achieve the correct shade. The lighter the color the more water that is required. Mix all colors in this way.

Dip an art brush in the thinned color. Wipe the brush on a paper towel, and then dry brush the color onto the gel-covered wafer paper picture. *Be sure not to dampen the wafer paper too much or the picture will curl.*

Using a black non-toxic marker, trace the verse onto another piece of wafer paper (p22). Allow to set. Apply gel over verse and allow to dry. When wafer papers are completely dry, invert them onto a sheet of wax paper or parchment paper and brush a thin coat of clear piping gel on the back. Carefully remove and place onto the iced cake, gel side down. Smooth out any bubbles with your fingers.

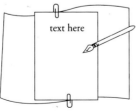

To complete the cake, cut ½ in (1.3cm) off the end of a parchment cone, insert tip #16, and half fill with white icing. Make a white zigzag border (p16) around the outside edges of the book, as shown. Place the yellow ribbon page finder down the center of the cake.

Victorian Doll

EQUIPMENT

1 – 9 in x 13 in (22.9cm x 33cm) cake pan
1 – 14 in (35.6cm) oval glass platter
serrated knife
small metal spatula
small piece of parchment paper
wafer (rice) paper
brown non-toxic pen
pastry brush
no.3 paint brush
5 parchment (greaseproof paper) cones:
  2 large, 3 medium
tips #233, #2, #3, #352, #14
coupler
paste colors (food coloring): green, copper,
  egg shade, yellow, brown, sky blue,
5 in (12.7cm) white paper doily
toothpicks
small plaid bow (optional)
patterns for doll and doll's face (p94)

INGREDIENTS		
1	2-layer cake mix or Never-Fail Chocolate Cake (p8)	1
	Buttercream Icing (p12)	
½ cup	copper	125ml
1 cup	pale pink	250ml
¼ cup	dark yellow	50ml
1 cup	dark green	250ml
½ cup	white	125ml
¼ cup	bright pink	50ml
¼ cup	light green	50ml
1 tbs	clear piping gel	15ml
17	copper drop flowers (p21)	17
25	pale pink drop flowers	25

The day before you decorate the cake, prepare 17 copper and 25 pale pink drop flowers. You will need extra parchment cones for this and tips #224, #231.

First day

Prepare the cake mix according to the instructions on the cake-mix package or use the Never-Fail Chocolate Cake recipe. Prepare the baking pan (p9).

Second day

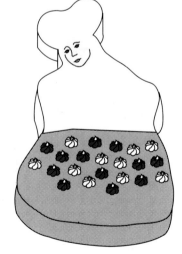

Add cake mixture and wrap the pan with baking strips (p9). Bake at 350°F (180°C) (gas or electric) for 25 to 30 minutes or until cake tests done (p9). Remove baking strips. Allow the cake to stand 5 to 7 minutes, then invert onto a wire rack to cool completely. Wrap and freeze cake.

Using the doll pattern, cut the frozen cake and attach it with a dab of icing to the cake platter.

Smooth a layer of dark green icing on the bottom half of the doll cake shape covering the sides as well. Use a small metal spatula to ice the cake. Ice the top portion and sides of the cake in the same way using the pale pink icing.

Allow the icings to dry. Smooth with parchment.

Using a brown non-toxic pen on wafer paper, trace the doll's face from the pattern. Brush the wafer paper with gel and paint in the traced features using paint brush and the paste colors. Use a dot of sky blue for the eyes,

a touch of copper for the flesh, and a hint of pink for blush on the cheeks. When dry, attach the painted face to the iced cake with the piping gel.

Set the prepared drop flowers (17 copper, 15 pink) across the middle section of the green coat. Cut ½ in (1.3cm) off the end of a parchment
Victorian Lady continued on p88.

cone and add tip #352. Pipe light green icing leaves to flowers. Add remaining pink drop flowers to the top portion of coat.

Cut ½ in (1.3cm) off the end of a large parchment cone, drop in tip #233. Add white icing for the fur trim on coat, gloves, muff, and bottom of skirt. Use small up and down strokes to create fur-like hairs.

Cut ½ in (1.3cm) off the end of another parchment cone, insert tip #3, and add dark yellow icing (use egg shade paste color). Begin at center front head and pull flat strands of icing out from the head to form hair. Then a tight "e" motion for ringlets down doll's neck.

While yellow icing is soft, add the folded white doily to the top of the doll's head for the bonnet.

Cut ½ in (1.3cm) off the end of a large parchment cone, drop in coupler, and half fill cone with bright pink icing. Attach tip #2. Draw the ribbons with a toothpick, as shown.

Outline with tip #2. Next outline the heart-shaped background with bright pink. Change to tip #14 and fill in ribbons with bright pink stars.

Cut ½ in (1.3cm) off the end of another cone, drop in tip #14 and add pale pink icing. Add fill-in stars to bonnet.

Wedding or Anniversary

EQUIPMENT

1 – 6-in (15.2-cm)-round cake pan
  3 in (7.6cm) deep
1 – 10-in (25.4-cm)-round cake pan
  3 in (7.6cm) deep
baking strips
2 wire racks
1 – 7-in (17.8-cm)-round separator plate
4 – 7 in (17.8cm) spike pillars
1 – 12-in (30.5-cm)-round cake plate
  or covered board (p10)
1 large parchment (greaseproof paper) cone
tips #2, #22, #352
1 coupler
scissors
wax paper
toothpicks
candy thermometer

	INGREDIENTS	
2	recipes Applesauce Cake (p8)	2
1	recipe pink Poured Fondant Icing (p12)	1
3 cups	Buttercream Icing	750ml
10	3-petal Buttercream Icing roses	10
14	5-petal Buttercream Icing roses	14

Prepare the Buttercream Icing roses the day before making the cake. You will need 24 – 1½-in (3.8-cm) -foil squares, a no.10 nail, and extra parchment cones and tip #104 for this.

Prepare the 2 recipes for Applesauce Cake together. Prepare the round pans (p9). Divide the mixture into the pans, filling them slightly over ⅔ full in order to achieve height for the cakes. Wrap pans with baking strips (p9). *(Use any leftover batter for cupcakes.)* Bake cakes at 350°F (180°C) (gas or electric) for 50 minutes for the 10-in cake and 30 minutes for the 6-in cake or until cakes test done (p9). Remove baking strips. Allow cakes to cool in pans for 7 to 10 minutes, then invert cakes onto wire racks to cool completely.

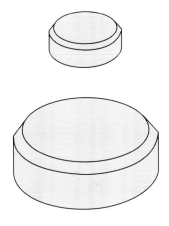

To achieve the rounded edge on cake tiers, use scissors to remove the top ½ in (1.3cm) crust edge on cakes. Be sure to cut on a slant, as shown. Set cake tiers on wire racks set on wax paper to catch the excess poured icing. Spilled icing can be reheated and used again.

Prepare Poured Fondant Icing and pour over cakes. Should your cakes require a second coat of fondant, be sure to allow the icing to set between coats. Reheat the leftover fondant to 100°F (37.7°C) before pouring.

Wedding or Anniversary continued on p90.

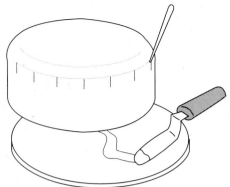

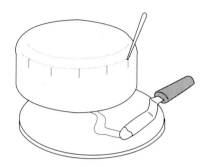

After the fondant has completely set, place the 10-in (25.4-cm)-round cake on the 12 in (30.5cm) plate and adhere with a little icing. Mark off 16 equal sections on side of cake with a toothpick to indicate where the border will go.

Center the 7-in (17.8-cm)-round separator plate on top of the 10-in (25.4-cm)-round iced cake. This will help you properly position the spike pillars. Remove the plate and insert the 4 spike pillars which will hold the top cake.

Use a dab of icing to attach the iced 6-in (15.2-cm)-round cake to the 7-in (17.8-cm)-round separator plate. With a toothpick mark top cake into 12 equal sections around side of cake to indicate where the scallop design will go, as shown.

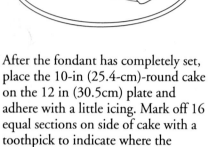

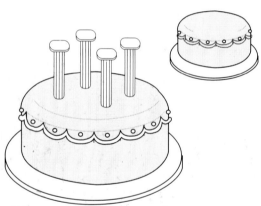

Cut 1 in (2.5cm) off a large parchment cone, insert a coupler and tip #2, and half fill cone with white Buttercream Icing. Pipe the scallop design on both cakes, as shown. Add center dot of icing to each scallop.

Place smaller cake on pillars. Change to tip #22. Complete large shell borders (p16) around the bottoms of both cakes.

Change to leaf tip #352. Place white Buttercream Icing roses on both cakes. Refer to the photograph for the placement. Pipe white leaves (p20), as shown in photograph.

Patterns for cutting out cake shapes or ornaments for cakes are on grids that use the following measure:

1 square = 1 inch or 2.5cm

Use a piece of lightweight cardboard or greaseproof paper and with pencil and ruler mark it with 1 in (2.5cm) squares. Draw the pattern on the new grid a square at a time. Cut out.

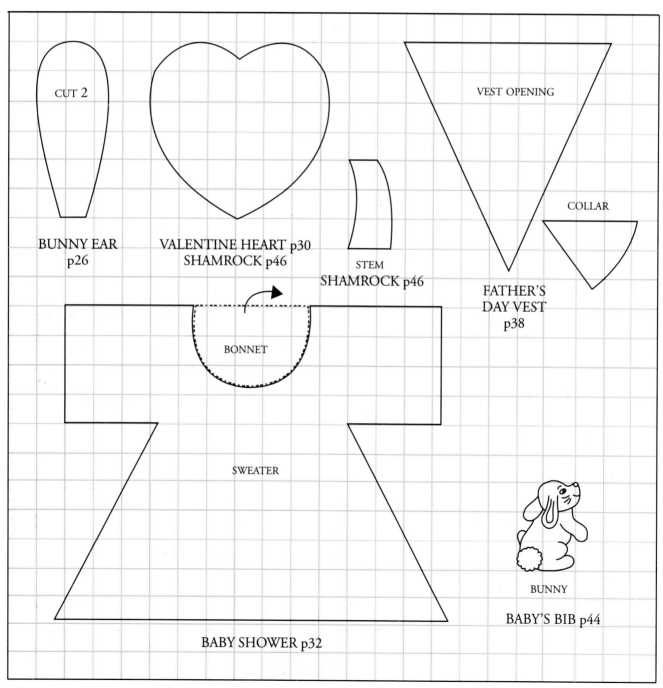

CUT 2

BUNNY EAR
p26

VALENTINE HEART p30
SHAMROCK p46

STEM
SHAMROCK p46

VEST OPENING

COLLAR

FATHER'S
DAY VEST
p38

BONNET

SWEATER

BUNNY

BABY'S BIB p44

BABY SHOWER p32

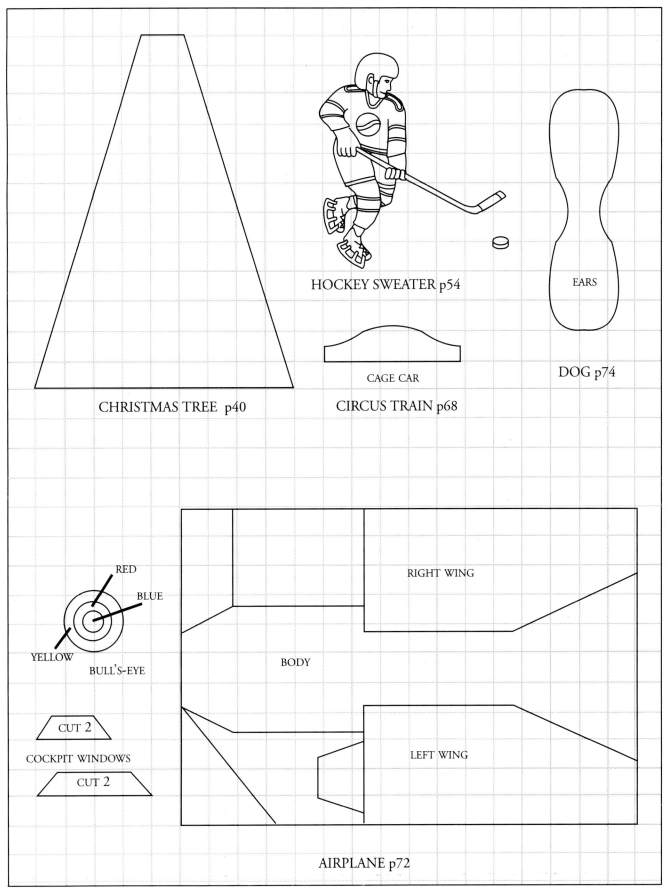

CHRISTMAS TREE p40

HOCKEY SWEATER p54

CAGE CAR

CIRCUS TRAIN p68

EARS

DOG p74

RED

BLUE

YELLOW

BULL'S-EYE

CUT 2

COCKPIT WINDOWS

CUT 2

RIGHT WING

BODY

LEFT WING

AIRPLANE p72

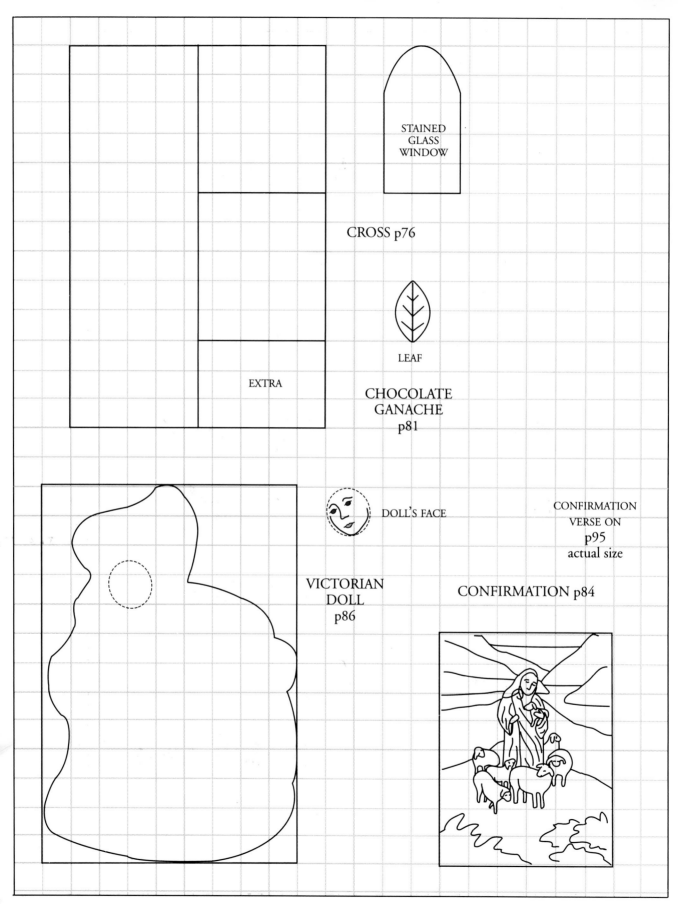

STAINED
GLASS
WINDOW

CROSS p76

LEAF

CHOCOLATE
GANACHE
p81

EXTRA

DOLL'S FACE

CONFIRMATION
VERSE ON
p95
actual size

VICTORIAN
DOLL
p86

CONFIRMATION p84

He shall feed his flock like a shepherd: he shall gather the lambs with his arm, and carry them in his bosom, and shall gently lead those that are with young.

Isaiah 40:11

ACTUAL SIZE

Index